AAL - 4547

THE MEGALITH BUILDERS OF
WESTERN EUROPE

GLYN DANIEL

THE MEGALITH BUILDERS
OF WESTERN EUROPE

GREENWOOD PRESS, PUBLISHERS
WESTPORT, CONNECTICUT

Library of Congress Cataloging in Publication Data

Daniel, Glyn Edmund.
   The megalith builders of Western Europe.

   Reprint. Originally published: London ; New York :
Hutchinson of London, c1958.
   Bibliography: p.
   Includes index.
   1. Megalithic monuments--Europe.   2. Europe--
Antiquities.   I. Title.
GN803.D36   1985   936   85-2578
ISBN 0-313-24836-2 (lib. bdg.)

© G. E. Daniel 1958, 1962

Reprinted with the permission of Glyn Edmund Daniel

Reprinted in 1985 by Greenwood Press
A division of Congressional Information Service, Inc.
88 Post Road West, Westport, Connecticut 06881

Printed in the United States of America

10 9 8 7 6 5 4 3 2 1

CONTENTS

PREFACE

WHEN Professor Hawkes invited me to write this book for the Archaeology Section of the *Hutchinson University Library*, I was happy to accept because it gave me an opportunity of summarizing my own views at the present moment on megalithic tombs in Europe, and seeing where and why they differed from views of other writers on this large and fascinating subject. I had attempted this once before, in my *Dual Nature of the Megalithic Colonisation of Prehistoric Europe* published in the *Proceedings of the Prehistoric Society* for 1941; but in the twenty years that have elapsed since I wrote that paper, I have learnt a lot more about megaliths, and, as is natural, find I disagree in many ways with what I said before.

Slowly we move on to firmer ground in the confusions and controversies that have surrounded megaliths since archaeologists began to think of them as a category for the first time in the early nineteenth century; their distribution in space and the extent of their morphological variety in Europe is gradually becoming known to us. The extension of Carbon 14 dating to megalithic monuments, just beginning, may in ten years give us some of the fixed points in megalithic chronology we so badly need.

At present then, this is just a short summary of some of the facts and ideas about megaliths in western Europe. I have tried to give different points of view while indicating the hypotheses which seem to me most useful. This book has been read in its entirety by Professor Stuart Piggott, Mr T. G. E. Powell, and the late Professor Séan ÓRíordáin, and I am grateful to them and to Professor Hawkes for their comments and suggestions. I have found the task of compressing even general views about a large subject into forty thousand words a difficult one; much has had to be omitted

9

and many things stated badly and abruptly which need arguing.

It is not possible to thank here all those who in discussion, travel, field-work, and excavation have helped me learn about megalithic monuments. My debt to my French friends and colleagues will be apparent in my *Prehistoric Chamber Tombs of France*, to be published next year. My special thanks are due to those who gave permission for drawings or photographs to be reproduced here, namely the Ministry of Works, The Controller of H.M. Stationery Office, Messrs Thames & Hudson, Messrs Routledge & Kegan Paul, Mrs E. M. Clifford, Professor Stuart Piggott, the Archives Photographiques of the Caisse Nationale des Monuments Historiques de France, and Messrs T. H. Mason, and to my wife who has drawn many of the maps and figures.

G. E. D.

Cambridge, May 1958

PREFACE TO SECOND EDITION

THE preface to the first edition of this book was written in May 1958 and contained this sentence: 'The extension of Carbon 14 dating to megalithic monuments, just beginning, may in ten years give us some of the fixed points in megalithic chronology we so badly need.' Now only four years later it is possible to say that Carbon 14 has already given us many new dates which demand fresh thinking about megalithic chronology as a whole. It is still too early· to assess these new dates in detail and present a new picture of megalithic chronology, but in a note added to the end of this book some brief consideration is given to them.

G. E. D.

March 1962

I

MEGALITHIC TOMBS AND TEMPLES

THERE can be very few interested students of early man in western Europe, or for that matter, very few well-travelled people in present-day western Europe who have not at some time or another seen the remains of a megalithic tomb – the 'dolmens' and 'cromlechs' and 'giants' graves' of popular parlance or of some non-sepulchral megalithic monument like a stone circle or a stone row. New Grange, Maes Howe, Stoney Littleton, the stone alignments at Carnac, the Déhus and La Hougue Bie in the Channel Islands, Stonehenge, and Avebury – these and many others are among the most famous of the antiquarian touristic curiosities of Europe. They are also the first surviving architectural monuments in north-western Europe and merit our special attention on that account alone. There were houses (and also perhaps ritual monuments of wood) built before the megalith builders spread through Atlantic Europe at a time which, as will be argued later, is probably somewhere in the first half of the second millennium B.C., but most of these houses were of wood, or wood, wattle, and daub, turves and thatch, and other similar perishable materials. These early houses usually only survive in the form of wooden post-holes which air photographs and excavations pick out in the soil, or as the stone footings of walls. Occasionally, as at Skara Brae in the Orkneys, where there was a shortage of suitable timber and a ready supply of stone that would split into flat slabs, houses and house furniture were built of stone and have survived to the present day to give us a glimpse of early domestic architecture. But Skara Brae is a rarity; the first buildings that survive in western Europe to give us at the present day some idea of the earliest architectural aspirations and ideals of prehistoric man in the British Isles, in France, and in the western Mediterranean, are the megalithic tombs and temples.

There is a sense in which all these monuments in western Europe – there must, at a guess be between forty and fifty thousand of them – can be grouped together and labelled megalithic, and that is that they all employ very large stones, or megaliths, in their construction. Some of the stones used in these monuments are very large indeed : the largest stone used in the great trilithon at Stonehenge was 29 feet 8 inches in length, and the great broken menhir at Locmariaquer in southern Brittany was, when intact, about 65 feet in height. The capstone of the Mount Browne dolmen, County Carlow in Ireland, is estimated as weighing about 100 tons; the great megalithic tomb of Bagneux near Saumur in central France measures internally 61 feet long by about 16 feet wide and from 8 feet 6 inches to 9 feet high : it is roofed by four capstones each about 2 feet thick, and the largest of these four capstones was estimated very accurately by Vice-Admiral Boyle Somerville to weigh just about 86 tons. This estimate was not guesswork but based on the dimensions of the great western capstone at Saumur, which is 23 feet square by 2 feet 4 inches thick, and the assumption that one cubic foot of the calcareous limestone out of which it is made weighed $156\frac{1}{2}$ lb. Without any doubt the word 'megalithic' is very properly applied to a great many of the prehistoric monuments which it is proposed to study in this book. It is a word derived from the Greek *megas*, great and *lithos*, stone, and was first used for these great stone structures in the period 1840–60. The only two books that exist in the English language which are entirely devoted to the study of megalithic monuments do not use the phrase megalith in their titles. These are James Fergusson's *Rude Stone Monuments in all Countries; their Age and Uses*, published in 1872, and T. E. Peet's *Rough Stone Monuments and their Builders*, which came out forty years later. These titles emphasize

another characteristic of megalithic architecture, namely
the fact that the great stones used are rarely dressed to
straight edges and faces; they are rough, rude stones. The
term megalith is the most useful general one because it
does emphasize what is to most people the first noticed
and most striking feature of these monuments, the use of
great stones, or even, as Professor Gordon Childe has put it,
the use of 'extravagantly large stones'.

It might be thought logical to apply the term 'megalithic'
to all constructions using very large roughly dressed slabs
of stone. The clapper bridges of Dartmoor, for example, are
megalithic monuments, and megaliths are used in some of
the Dartmoor pounds, and in the field walls of Cornwall
and Scilly. It is possible to find modern pigsties in Pembrokeshire which ought to be classified as megaliths. But in
archaeology it is customary to restrict the term megalithic
monument to certain specific types of construction em-
ploying these large stones – chamber tombs, rows, single
standing stones, and enclosures – which were, in the main,
constructed between 2000 and 1500 B.C., and our concern
in this short book is with the people who built these great
stone monuments between three and four thousand years
ago.

It is convenient to distinguish, for the sake of description
and analysis, three separate types of prehistoric megalithic
monument in western Europe, namely :

1. the chamber tomb;
2. the single standing stone; and
3. the grouped standing stones.

In the first class, the chamber tomb or megalithic chamber,
we are dealing with a room or chamber – usually something large enough to walk into. The chamber of Cueva de
Menga in southern Spain, for example, is over 75 feet long
by 18 feet broad by 9 feet high; we have already quoted the
size of the great Bagneux chamber tomb in France. The
chamber tomb of New Grange in Ireland consists of a passage 62 feet long leading to a cruciform chamber 19 feet

6 inches high. These are fine exceptional monuments – the glories of the architectural traditions of the chamber-tomb builders. Many chamber tombs, however, are very much smaller and it is very difficult to distinguish some from what are usually called large stone cists. This word comes from the Welsh *cistvaen* meaning a box of stone, and is usually applied to a slab-lined grave set in the ground with a covering slab and large enough to hold only a single burial. Sometimes these cists are built on the surface of the ground and intermediate forms exist between cists and small megalithic chambers. But on the whole this wide range of size merely emphasizes the variety of construction within the tradition of building megalithic chamber tombs. All of them are buildings of walls and a roof and were essentially built to contain something, and, as years of archaeological research have proved, that something was the unburnt or burnt dead bodies of a community or family.

The second class of megalithic monuments we are distinguishing in western Europe consists of a single standing stone; usually called a menhir, from the Welsh words *maen*, stone, and *hir*, long. A special type of single standing stone is called a *llech* (again the Welsh and Breton word for stone) and is most common in Brittany. The third class, the group of standing stones, is difficult to particularize and includes many different kinds of megalithic monument. In western Britain there are many circles of stones like the Nine Maidens in Cornwall, or Long Meg and her Daughters in Cumberland, which seem to consist only of a circle of spaced stones. Then in many parts of Great Britain there are other circular groupings of megaliths forming an integral part of a monument with a bank and a ditch such as Avebury and Stonehenge itself; these embanked stone circles are themselves part of a category of prehistoric monument that is now generally referred to as a *henge* monument. Avebury has a great avenue of megaliths leading to it; Dartmoor has many much smaller stone avenues or rows leading to megalithic cists or, apparently,

to nothing at all, while in the Carnac region of southern Brit.
Brittany are the world-famous alignments comprising
nearly three thousand menhirs and extending for a distance
of three and a half to four miles. Some of these Carnac
alignments end in semicircular or semi-rectangular enclosures of menhirs. There is such variety about the
grouped standing stones that we must postpone discus-

Fig. 1 – Isometric view of Stonehenge by Stuart Piggott (1950)

sion of them until we have first discussed the chamber
tombs.

These are not hard-and-fast categories because menhirs
are often found associated with chamber tombs, as point-
ers perhaps, or crowning the top of a chambered barrow,
and some megalithic chamber tombs have around them
free-standing circles of stone. As we have mentioned, the
Dartmoor alignments (or some of them) are connected with
stone cists, while the Carnac alignments seem unconnected
with megalithic tombs, except that it is impossible to believe that all the megalithic monuments of southern Brittany are not in the end part of some great cultural and
religious unity of ideas and practice. There is another sense

in which the megalithic chambers should be distinguished in discussion from the structures of grouped megaliths forming circles and alignments. There is very little doubt, as we shall see in the next chapter, that the chambers are tombs, although earlier generations of antiquaries postulated many non-sepulchral usages for them. It also seems likely that most of the non-chambered megalithic monuments in western Europe are not tombs but temples, or, to use a cautious circumlocution, non-domestic and non-sepulchral sites of a ritual or sacred nature. This is not to say that there was no ritual in the use and construction of the chamber tombs; there was indeed, and, as we shall see, some of the tombs give us glimpses of the ideas that lay behind the ritual of funeral and entombment. Nor is it true to say that there is no dispute about whether some megalithic structures, like the enormous structures in Malta and Gozo, usually called 'temples', are really tombs or temples. It is just to say that as a useful basis for discussion in the present state of our knowledge about the megaliths of western Europe we can distinguish the megalithic sepulchral chambers on the one hand, and the megalith sacred sites or temples on the other.

Of course, some have argued that if prehistoric megalithic monuments appear to include structures as varied as small chamber tombs on the one hand and Avebury, Stonehenge, and the Carnac alignments on the other, it might be wondered whether they form a useful grouping for discussion at all. The answer is that they do because, superficially at least, to the general student of prehistoric monuments there is something in common, namely the use of large stones, and the use of large stones in techniques which do not involve dressing to fine surfaces and straight edges. There are exceptions to this; the sarsen stones at Stonehenge are one exception, and many of the stones in the megalithic 'temples' of Malta are another; but these monuments are exceptional megalithic structures and can only be understood as *tours de force* in the traditions of megalithic architecture, traditions which are based fundamentally on the use of roughly dressed large stones as walling and roofing stones.

These traditions differ essentially from what may conveniently be referred to as cyclopean architecture. The dictionary often makes no distinction between megalithic and cyclopean techniques of construction. Both, admittedly, use large stones, but it is convenient to use the term cyclopean architecture where the large slabs are placed one on top of the other as in the *navetas* of the Balearics, the *nuraghi* of Sardinia, or the walls of Tarragona, for example. The essentials of megalithic construction are either the single large slab or the large slab as walling stone with another large slab resting on two or more large walling stones as a capstone – a sort of house of cards architecture. Both megalithic and cyclopean architecture differ in detail from the stone-work of the great Aegean *tholoi* which is chisel-dressed and sometimes saw-cut. Now there are all sorts of intermediate monuments that are constructionally difficult to fit into these three categories, but they do form useful categories against which to discuss the early architecture of Europe – the megalithic monuments of mainly western and north-western Europe, the cyclopean monuments which are very common in the Mediterranean, and the chisel-dressed ashlar monuments of mainly the east Mediterranean.

Whatever may be the details of the construction of megalithic monuments in western Europe, and however various may be the form of the monuments built with these great stones, they all pose to the present-day student of prehistoric archaeology the problem of how these large stones were obtained and handled. Some megalithic monuments, like the chamber tomb of Barclodiad y Gawres in Anglesey, are constructed out of large glacial erratics, found locally. Others are made of local rock outcropping near by, and some of this stone must have been quarried. Near the chamber tomb of Tinkinswood near Cardiff in south Wales is an outcrop of limestone from which the stone walling and roofing of the tomb have come; this outcrop is pitted with shallow surface quarrying and it is by no means impossible that this represents the actual quarry from which prehistoric man obtained his large stones. A similar quarry site, with shallow surface stripping of large stones, is to be seen in the Burren country of county Clare in west Ireland. It is likely, as it is reasonable, that the great majority of the large stones used in building megaliths was obtained locally, but there are a few examples of the long-distance transport of megaliths. The stones used in building the chamber tomb of Moulins near Châteauroux in central France came from a geological formation outcropping no nearer than thirty miles.

The foreign or blue stones at Stonehenge are the classic example of the long-distance transport of large stones. The stones of which Stonehenge is built are of two kinds: the sarsens, and the blue stones. The sarsens, which include all the very big stones, are the remains of a cap of Tertiary sandstone which once covered Salisbury Plain. Sarsens, or 'grey wethers' as they are often called, can still be found in north Wiltshire, particularly along the Marlborough Downs. The foreign or blue stones which comprise the smaller circle and smaller horseshoe at Stonehenge are of rocks that do not occur locally as outcrops or glacial erratics in southern Britain. The researches of Dr H. H. Thomas in the early twenties showed that the only place where all the foreign stones found at Stonehenge occurred naturally together was Pembrokeshire, and it is now generally accepted that the blue stones of Stonehenge came from the east end of the Presely mountains – which is 140 miles as the crow flies from Stonehenge. Various routes have been suggested by which these megaliths could have been moved from Pembrokeshire to Salisbury Plain: and all-land route crossing the Severn near Gloucester is about 180 miles, by sea to the Mendips and then by land is about 150 miles, whereas a long sea route round Cornwall and then up the Hampshire Avon – a possible route suggested by O. G. S. Crawford – is about 400 miles. Whatever route was used, the transport of the blue stones is a remarkable technical

18

achievement; it is, as far as we know, the only such very long-distance transport of stones used in building a megalith monument. Detailed petrological study of other monuments may reveal other equally surprising feats of transportation. The transport of the blue stones to Stonehenge, though at present a unique event, only serves to emphasize the technical problems involved in megalithic construction and the technical achievements of the megalith builders.

We can point to what may well be the quarries of the megalith builders, and we can with certainty indicate that they sometimes transported stones for considerable distances, but we are still in the dark about their techniques of quarrying, of moving, and of erecting these great stones. We can get some sort of information by studying the techniques used at the present day in parts of the world such as Assam or Africa where megalithic monuments are still made, and from the difficulties which modern farmers have had in trying to break up megalithic monuments. Somewhere between 1830 and 1840 the main capstone of a megalithic chamber tomb near Saumur in central France was moved to be used as a bridge across a river. Eighteen pairs of oxen were required to drag the capstone, and enormous rollers – each made of the trunks of four oak trees lashed together – each roller having a circumference of over a metre.

In Japan megalithic tombs were constructed well into historic times and written sources survive about them. The Emperor Kôtoku in the middle of the seventh century A.D. prohibited the building of great stone tombs in Japan because of the waste of labour involved. A detailed study has been made of the construction of the Japanese megalithic tomb of Ishibutai; this is by no means the largest of the Japanese megaliths. It had a rectangular chamber 25 feet by 11 feet by 15 feet high approached by a passage 38 feet in length, and roofed by two capstones each weighing between 60 and 70 tons. Professor Takahashi, who was Professor of Engineering in the University of Kyoto, made calculations as to how the monument was constructed. His

19

explanation of how the big stones were moved and set up involves the stones being dragged on sledges and rollers, earthen banks up which the dragging could take place, raising the stones by means of radiating levers and weights, and dropping the large stones into prepared trenches revetted with wood. Professor Takahashi estimated that, taking all circumstances into account, the construction of the Ishibutai tomb must have occupied betweeen 300 and 400 men a whole year.

Some comparable calculations have been made about the construction of megalithic monuments in the British Isles. When Mr Alexander Keiller was excavating Avebury, he was much intrigued by the problem of how the megaliths were set up. He and his staff had to erect many megaliths that had fallen down or been deliberately buried in the seventeenth century. In 1934 Mr Keiller experimented by putting up an average-sized stone with no other equipment than what he thought would be available to prehistoric people in the first quarter of the second millennium B.C. The result was that one skilled foreman – a man who had had considerable experience of the re-erection of megaliths at Stonehenge previously – and twelve inexperienced workmen succeeded in putting up the stone in five days. The experiment was taken to show that one hundred men could have erected one hundred megaliths in about two months. This is, of course, an entirely mathematical calculation and presupposes that the stones had been placed by their stone-holes in advance. It does, however, very clearly emphasize the effort involved in constructing megaliths; this simple calculation should be remembered together with the fact that the great Carnac alignments contain nearly three thousand stones. Keiller's idea was that the main technique of construction involved wooden stakes, timber baulks, and rawhide ropes.

It is not without interest in our present discussion to recollect the manoeuvres of that extraordinary man Giovanni Belzoni, when he removed the colossal head of Rameses II from the Ramesseum on the first stages of its journey to the British Museum. It weighed eight tons; Belzoni's sole equipment was fourteen poles, four palm-leaf ropes, and four rollers. He had no tackle of any kind yet he succeeded in moving this heavy statue, although in the first four days he achieved only 150 yards.[1] Also of interest are the experiments which Thor Heyerdal, of *Kon-Tiki* fame, conducted in 1956 on Easter Island. He organized the transport of one of the great statues and erected it without any mechanical aids by what he believed were the original techniques. A team of 180 Easter Islanders dragged a 30-ton statue from its quarry to where it was to be erected; they raised it by first levering and then hauling it to the vertical by ropes. Twelve islanders raised the statue to the vertical in eighteen days.

When we consider some of the mounds or barrows of earth and stone that incorporate the chamber tombs of north-western Europe, we get another extraordinary impression of the labour involved in their construction. The late Professor Gordon Childe once calculated that some of the funerary barrows on the barren moors of Caithness contained 135,000 cubic feet or 8,000 tons of stone – enough to build five reasonably sized parish churches! Childe's calculations were based on a barrow of 240 feet long: the West Kennet and East Kennet long barrows in north Wiltshire are considerably longer and larger.

Mrs E. M. Clifford has made an interesting calculation about the construction of the Rodmarton long barrow in Gloucestershire. She estimates that the cairn contains at least 5,000 tons of stone, and writes:

> The stones in the body of the cairn are placed with some care, not thrown in haphazardly. Not more than twenty men could do this at one time. This would employ twenty men placing, twenty men carrying, forty men digging, and twenty directors, foremen and those engaged on ancillary activities – a total of 100. If each of

1. I quote these details from C. Clair, *Strong Man Egyptologist*, 1957, pp. 46–7.

The Megalith Builders of Western Europe

the forty men digging won half a ton of stone a day 250 working days would be needed to provide 5,000 tons of stone, or one year with stoppages for weather, festivals, rest, etc., and another year for the preparation of site and erection of megaliths, which would involve the continuous employment of 100 men for two years in all.[1]

There is no need now to give any further examples to emphasize the size and complexity of the megalithic monuments of western Europe. Their construction, and certainly the construction of the finest and biggest of them, was a great labour, the details of which we can but dimly apprehend. But when we discuss the origins of these megalithic monuments it is important to remember these constructional points. When we are concerned with distributions and sequences of tomb-plans and with the objects of dateable type buried with the dead in these tombs, it is easy to forget the implications in human terms of these great monuments – the man hours of navvying and quarrying and dragging involved, and the ideas and ideals that prompted and inspired this hard work.

We have referred to megalithic monuments in other parts of the world than western Europe, which is our concern here. The distribution of megalithic monuments in western Europe is shown in the map (Fig. 2, p. 26). Outside these areas there are, in the Mediterranean–Black Sea belt of the old world, megalithic monuments in north Africa, especially in Algeria; there are megalithic tombs in Bulgaria, in Palestine, and in Caucasia. South of Mediterranean Africa megalithic structures are known from Abyssinia and the Sudan. Megalithic structures are reported from Persia, from Baluchistan and Kashmir, but undoubtedly one of the main concentrations of megalithic structures in the world is central and south India. The megalithic monuments of the Deccan, many of which have porthole devices resemb-

1. Mrs E. M. Clifford in Fox and Dickins (editors), *The Early Cultures of North-Western Europe*, 1950, p. 35.

Megalithic Tombs and Temples

ling some of the similar devices in western European megalithic tombs, have been known about for a very long time, but in the last decade systematic researches, particularly the excavations carried out by Sir Mortimer Wheeler in Mysore State, have much enlarged our knowledge of them and dated them – or at least some of them – to the period c. 200 B.C. to A.D. 50 – the period of the Early Iron Age in southern India. There are megaliths in Assam and Sumatra and in some Polynesian islands like Malekula. We have already referred to some of the Japanese megaliths; these seem to date from the period of at most a millennium lasting from the two centuries before the Christian era to the seventh century A.D. Finally, there are monuments using megaliths in Central America and in the north of South America.

Discussion on the origin and interrelations of these megalithic monuments has only become possible, naturally, as their existence and distribution was gradually appreciated. It was the European megalithic monuments that were first known about. As early as 1864 the French archaeologist Alexandre Bertrand argued that megalithic monuments in Europe were all built by one people who spread from north to south; and the following year, when the Baron de Bonstetten published his famous *Essai sur les dolmens*, he advocated the same point of view. In 1872 General Faidherbe drew the attention of archaeologists to the Algerian megalithic monuments; he too maintained that all megalithic monuments from Africa to northern Europe were the work of one people who moved southwards from the Baltic. In this same year James Fergusson published his *Rude Stone Monuments in all Countries*. He had become interested in megaliths as part of his general study of architecture, and was convinced that they all were part of one stylistic phase of architectural history. Fergusson confessed that up to 1872 'no royal road has been discovered which leads to an explanation of our megalithic antiquities', but was nevertheless convinced of one thing, that the style of architecture to which these monuments

23

belong is a style, like Gothic, Grecian, Egyptian, Buddhist or any other' and that the megalithic monuments of the world 'were generally erected by partially civilized races after they had come into contact with the Romans, and most of them may be considered as belonging to the first ten centuries of the Christian Era'.

Fergusson's dating was not accepted by many archaeologists, but his idea of architectural style rather than a migrating people as the linking factor was widely canvassed. De Mortillet, in 1874, at the Stockholm Congress of Prehistoric Archaeology, put forward the view that megalithic monuments in different parts of the world were due to the work of different people with different cultures, and that what was diffused over the world was the custom of building such monuments and not the builders themselves. This idea of the spread of what may be termed a megalithic 'influence' was widely canvassed at the end of the nineteenth century, most people bringing this influence from the east Mediterranean or Asia, while Salomon Reinach reversed it and sent it eastwards from France.

In the present century the problem of the diffusion of megalithic monuments can be seen best against the general study of the diffusion of culture to which archaeologists and anthropologists have given so much thought. Professor T. Eric Peet, when he wrote his *Rough Stone Monuments* forty years after James Fergusson, discusses the megalithic 'influence' or megalithic 'style' idea, but rejects it. After very careful consideration he says, 'it thus seems the most probable theory of the origin of the megalithic monuments is that this style of building was brought to the various countries in which we find it by a single race in an immense migration or series of migrations'. While advocating this view, Peet was unable to decide whence this migrating 'race' came from; the east, northern Europe, and Africa were all considered and the sad negative conclusion arrived at that 'it is probable that the problem will never be solved'. Sir Grafton Elliot Smith and his pupil, W. J. Perry, who between them spent a lifetime in advocating that civilization was due to the spread of a master-race from Egypt, rapidly and easily incorporated the megalithic monuments of the world in their thesis.

Archaeologists and anthropologists have not unnaturally reacted against the monocentric hyper-diffusionism of the Elliot Smith–Perry school, and there are not many who to-day regard the megalithic monuments of the world as remains of wandering Egyptians. Nor is it possible to speak of a megalithic race, if the word race is used, as it should be, in its strict physical – anthropological connotation of a group of people with heritable physical characteristics in common. The physical types associated with megaliths and buried in them differ widely, as we shall see, even in a small area like western Europe. But if we set aside the extravagances of a megalithic race in the physical sense, and what seems to most people the extravagancy of the migrating Children of the Sun from Egypt, there remains the question, are the megalithic monuments of the world the result of the spread of people (or influences) from one centre, or are they not?

Recently the problem and this question has been put into fresh perspective by Wheeler's excavations in southern India, and by Gordon Childe's discussion of the Indian megaliths in relation to those of Europe and south-west Asia. It is indeed possible, though not proved, that the port-holed cists of the Indian Deccan are derived from those of western Asia, despite the disparities of time and place; but this does not necessarily imply world connexions between all megaliths. Others have argued that there is very little in common between the structures in different parts of the world designated as megaliths, save the use of large stones, and that this use of large stones might well have arisen independently in different parts of the world. What is most important, as students of the theory of material culture are always emphasizing, is that we should not assume a connexion between two traits in two cultures unless we can prove that the traits are formally, constructionally, and functionally identical, and can demonstrate the

25

chronological and geographical possibilities of connexion. It is by no means impossible that megaliths originated in southern Europe and spread to India, Indonesia, and Japan;

Fig. 2 – Distribution map of megalithic monuments in western Europe

but before we can assess the different points of view about the unity or disunity of megaliths, we need careful analyses of the structures in different regions.

Here our concern is with the west European megaliths, and we turn first and mainly to the megalithic chambers. The non-sepulchral monuments have a restricted distribution in western Europe, and are best seen when we have accumulated facts about the burial chambers. The megalithic collective tombs occur, as can be seen from the map (Fig. 2), in the central and western Mediterranean, in Iberia, France, the British Isles, and in north Germany, Holland, Denmark, and south Sweden. This map is called the distribution of megalithic chamber tombs in western Europe, but it must be realized at once that it includes tombs identical in function and form with megalithic tombs but constructed in a different way. In south-eastern Spain identical tombs are built entirely of dry-walling and roofed by corbelling; many of the prehistoric collective tombs in Sardinia and the Balearics are cyclopean and not megalithic in construction, and in Sicily and the Tagus estuary area of Portugal, for example, rock-cut tombs exactly parallel in form those built with megaliths. And as we shall see there are in parts of southern Spain and France, prehistoric collective tombs that, from the constructional point of view, are half-way between being cut in the rock and built up on the surface of the ground. So, already, while we may talk loosely about megalithic tombs and temples in western Europe, in reality we should be talking of prehistoric collective tombs, and recognizing that tombs which strictly justify the description 'megalithic' are only one constructional variety in a larger class.

Indeed, the right way at the outset to place our problems in proper perspective is to say that the prehistoric megalithic monuments of western Europe are of various kinds, among which chamber tombs and circular temples are the most simple and well-known categories, but that each of these two categories merely forms part of a wider category – prehistoric collective tombs, and prehistoric circular temples. Many of the prehistoric circular temples are megalithic; others are megaxylic and used large pieces of wood. Many of the prehistoric chamber tombs are megalithic; many are not. It is only by realizing this point very clearly from the beginning that we can permit ourselves to talk about the megalith builders of prehistoric Europe, to approach an understanding of how megalith building came into being in Europe, and how megalithic architecture cannot be studied in isolation on a European or world basis but only in relation to the monuments built with megaliths and the societies that built them.

2

THE PREHISTORIC COLLECTIVE TOMBS OF
WESTERN EUROPE

WE have already, in the last chapter, briefly indicated where in Europe the prehistoric collective tombs are to be found, and the distribution is shown graphically in the map (Fig. 2, p. 26). We have also indicated that there are two main methods of constructing these prehistoric burial chambers :

1. by building them up on the surface of the ground – the *cryptes dolmeniques* of French writers, and the built-up or surface tombs of English writers; and
2. by excavating them in the ground – the *grottes sépulchrales artificielles* of French archaeologists and the rock-cut tombs of English archaeologists.

The built-up or surface tombs may have some rock-cut features, such as a shallow rock-cut pit in which the walling stones of the chamber are set, and built-up tombs may occasionally utilize outcropping rock surfaces in part of their construction; but normally the built-up tomb is entirely on the surface of the ground, and consists of walls and a flat or corbelled roof. The rock-cut tomb may sometimes utilize features more normal to surface tombs; sometimes the tomb is cut in a sloping hillside or near the top of the ground surface and the highest part of the cut roof is a hole closed by a megalithic slab.

Apart from these intermediate features in rock-cut and surface tombs, we should distinguish, on constructional grounds, two further types of prehistoric chamber tomb in western Europe, which for convenience of reference we may call the *intermediate* type of chamber tomb, and the *sub-megalithic* type of chamber tomb. We will discuss these types after we have described the more normal types of tomb. The rock-cut collective tombs are well represented in Sicily, in the Balearics, and in parts of southern Iberia – especially in the lower valley of the Tagus (Fig. 3). The entrance to these rock-cut tombs is usually closed with

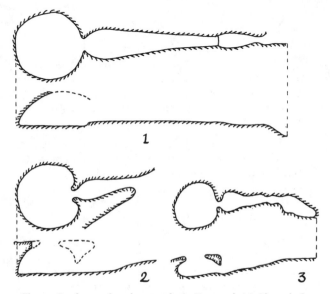

Fig. 3 – Rock-cut chamber tombs in Portugal. (1) Alapraia I. (2) Palmella III. (3) Carenque III (*after de Jalhay*)

special stones – the *pierres de fermeture* of French text-books – and blocking to prevent robbers and wild animals getting into the tombs, and perhaps also to prevent the spirits of the dead from getting out. It is perfectly true that the rock-cut tomb occurs in western Europe in areas where the cutting of the rock was an easy method of construction, but it is not arguable, as Elliot Smith held, that the distribution of rock-cut and surface tombs is entirely a function of local geology; for surface tombs do occur in areas where the soft rock makes rock-cut tombs possible. Such areas are the Charente department of western France and the north Wiltshire Downs. Local geology is a permissive, not a mandatory factor, in the selection of techniques for constructing tombs.

The surface tombs are far more widespread than the rock-cut tombs. They are walled with megaliths set on edge, forming *orthostats*, or by dry walling, or by a combination of orthostats and dry walling, or sometimes they are walled by large stones set one on top of another – the constructional technique we have already referred to as cyclopean. The combination of orthostats and dry-stone walling is a two-fold combination; the dry-stone walling is intercalary and fills in the interstices between the edges of the roughly dressed orthostats, or the dry-stone walling acts as a backing to the orthostats, rides over them, and binds them into a joint wall of orthostats and masonry. This latter form of construction is often referred to as the 'classic' form of megalithic construction; but it sometimes happens that the orthostats are not bonded into the wall and form a non-functional screen in front of the constructional dry walling.

The roofing of these surface chambers is formed by a large megalithic slab or capstone resting directly on the walls (whether they be orthostats, dry walling, or a combination of both walling techniques) or it is formed by corbelling. The technique of corbelling consists of small stones placed one on top of the other, each succeeding course over-sailing the one below until the area to be roofed can be bridged by one slab. Corbelling is essentially false vaulting, and the true vault or dome is not found in prehistoric collective tombs. The technique of corbelling to roof a building was know in Mesopotamia in prehistoric times and the true arch was known there as early as about 3000 B.C. – there are true domes in the Royal Tombs at Ur, but the true arch principle with wedge-shaped bricks and keystones to hold the whole arch in position was not known in Europe until Roman times.

The Megalith Builders of Western Europe

Very good examples of the corbel-roofed surface tombs are shown by New Grange in Ireland and Maes Howe in the Orkneys (Figs. 20 and 21, pp. 113 and 117). Indeed, an analysis of the construction of New Grange really emphasizes the general descriptive points already made. The passage at New Grange is a classic megalithic wall supporting large capstones; some, but not all, of the orthostats lining the passage serve as constructional props to the roofing stones. The average height of the passage is somewhere between five and seven feet: as the chamber is approached the roof gets higher and the chamber itself is roofed by a splendid, rather steep, corbelled vault, the top of which is 19 feet 6 inches above ground level. Maes Howe is a partly destroyed monument: indeed, we have a good idea when this very splendid tomb was destroyed, because its walls bear inscriptions in runes and also three engraved figures (a dragon, a walrus, and a serpent knot) executed in the twelfth century. Most of the runic inscriptions have been deciphered; they record personal names and statements of Vikings on their way to the Crusades, breaking into the Howe, and their removal thence of treasure. The central chamber in Maes Howe is 15 feet square; the walls of dry walling rise vertically for the first 4½ feet and then converge in overlapping courses – the original structure still surviving to 12 feet 6 inches. The corbelled vault at Maes Howe, when complete, must have been a very wonderful thing; like New Grange it was a splendid piece of architecture.

In a few rare examples the rock-cut tombs have some slight covering of earth or stones on top of them; one good example is that from Mallorca shown in the top drawing in Fig. 14 (p. 93). It is very common, however, for the surface tombs to be covered with and incorporated in a mound of earth and stones. To this funerary covering mound the French give the word *tumulus*, whereas we in the British Isles usually refer to it as a barrow, or a cairn, according to whether it is made of earth or stones. It seems most convenient when writing in English to refer to these mounds generally as barrows whatever they are made of. They are not merely covering mounds; often the heaping-up of earth and stones is necessary to keep together and revet and buttress the structure of the chamber. But it is not possible to argue that in all cases the barrow element of the surface collective tombs is purely constructional or functional; often the barrow itself has attained an importance of its own, and its size is out of all proportion to the functional and constructional reason for its existence. New Grange itself is a good example of this: the chamber and passage take up only a small part of the great circular barrow of over 250 feet in circumference in which it is set. In the Cotswold–Severn group of chambered long barrows in southern Britain there are many examples of this importance of the barrow *per se*: the average length of the barrows in this group is 150 feet and the average breadth 65 feet. Yet in this group the West Kennet long barrow is 320 to 340 feet in length and East Kennet as much as 350 feet. The known burial chamber in the West Kennet long barrow is only some 45 feet in length; the existence of a burial chamber in the East Kennet long barrow is only a matter of supposition, but in both these examples it is difficult to imagine that the length and size of these barrows bears any constructional and functional relationship to the necessity of covering over, protecting, and revetting the burial chamber.

In form, the barrows covering the surface burial chambers vary a great deal; a standard form covering great numbers of surface chamber tombs in Iberia, France, western Britain, Ireland, Scotland, and Scandinavia is the round barrow. Many of the elongated rectangular chambers in the Balearics, Sardinia, France, and the British Isles have ovate and long barrows, whereas in Scandinavia rectangular barrows are very common. But whatever the form of the barrow, it must not be supposed that they are haphazard accumulations of earth and stone. They are often carefully constructed, and sometimes it is possible to see differences in construction between different gangs of workmen; the barrow has revetting walls, and often carefully constructed extra-revetment material. Where the barrow is large, the entrance to the burial chamber is often a carefully defined area, forming a forecourt, with incurving walls. Fig. 9 (p. 64) is a drawing by Dr Georg Leisner, who has spent years studying the collective tombs of southern Iberia; it gives some idealized idea of what one of

Fig. 4 – The megalithic tomb of Bryn Celli Ddu in the mid nineteenth century. (From *Archaeologia Cambrensis*, vol. ii, 1847)

the tombs in south-east Spain might have looked like when its construction was completed, but it should be remembered that probably after the site had been used as a tomb most of the walls would have been hidden, and the forecourt and entrance filled in.

Some surface tombs at the present day are completely free of any barrow; they are what is described as freestanding burial chambers. Others are completely hidden in a barrow as we have seen, and these are all variations between the free-standing and completely covered monuments. The free-standing burial chamber is no rarity, and about a quarter of all the burial chambers in England and

34

Wales are free-standing. In the nineteenth century and earlier, when great controversies raged about the actual nature of these burial chambers, many antiquaries took the free-standing burial chamber to be an original form, whilst others argued that such monuments were merely the accidental remains of monuments ravaged by time, man, and nature. It was assumed by these latter antiquaries that all burial chambers were originally covered with mounds of earth and stones, and this is nowadays the most widely accepted view, except that in some areas, like the Burren country of County Clare in Ireland and parts of southern Spain, for example, it does not seem as if the burial chambers ever had mounds over them. The nineteenth-century drawing of Bryn Celli Ddu in Anglesey reproduced here (Fig. 4) is interesting in that it shows a chambered barrow in an advanced state of denudation. Most of the passage and chamber are visible, but there are traces of barrow around the feet of the stones, and some of the original barrow survives on the capstone.[1]

In the published sectional drawings of some chambered barrows it would appear that the barrow is constructed on ground level, and the chamber itself considerably above ground level and entirely in the body of the mound. This is almost certainly an illusion due to faulty observation and surveying, as may easily happen when a chambered barrow caps a hill and the spread skirts of the barrow are mistaken for its original level.[2]

We have already briefly mentioned two further constructional types of prehistoric collective tombs in western Europe, which we have referred to as *intermediate* and *submegalithic* tombs, and we have defined the former as being half-way between rock-cut and surface tombs. Good examples of this interesting constructional variant are the

1. Compare this drawing with the plans and photographs published by W. J. Hemp following his excavations in 1925–9 (*Archaeologia*, LXXXIII, pp. 179 ff.).

2. Minninglow was drawn in this way and so were all Macalister's sections of the Carrowkeel cemetery.

three splendid tombs near Antequera in southern Spain in
the province of Malaga, which go by the names of Cueva
de Menga, Cueva de Viera, and the Cueva de Romeral.
These three tombs are all built into natural hills, and it
appears that the builders first cut into natural hillocks until
they obtained a level floor of rock. They then set up their
orthostats in a shallow trench of the rock, or (as with the
Cueva de Romeral) faced the side of the trench they had
cut in the hill with dry walling, then roofed over the passage and chambers, re-formed the natural hill, and shaped
the hill to make it look like a round barrow. This is certainly an economical way of constructing a collective
tomb, but these great tombs at Antequera are no impoverished versions of the megalithic tombs we are discussing.
Indeed, they are some of the finest and most 'megalithic' of
tombs known in western Europe; Cueva de Menga itself
has a chamber 48 feet long with an extreme width of 16
feet and its greatest height of 10 feet. Perhaps the natural
hillocks were selected to save labour on mound construction and facilitate the erection of especially large and
impressive tombs. It is interesting that the four great capstones roofing the chamber of Cueva de Menga are supported not only by the walling orthostats but by three
great megalithic pillars in the centre. Pillars have been suggested to have existed in other megalithic tombs – sometimes wooden pillars; and, of course, the extent of the use
of such perishable substances as wood in the construction
of megalithic tombs is entirely a matter of speculation, but
must never be forgotten.

The small group of tombs not far from Arles in the south
of France, in the department of Bouches-du-Rhône and
usually known as the Fontvieille *Grottes*, show interesting
intermediate forms of construction. One of them, the
famous Grotte des Fées (or L'Épée de Roland as it is sometimes called) is cut entirely in the rock; three neighbouring
tombs, the Grotte Bounias, Grotte de la Source, and the
Grotte Castellet, are cut in the rock in much the same
way, and their walls are formed by the face of the rock,

36

but the roofs of these three tombs consist of large megalithic capstones resting on the natural rock and covered
over with mounds. Near by again is the fifth member of
the group, the Dolmen de Coutignargue, which is entirely
a surface tomb walled and roofed with megaliths. In the
Paris Basin in north France there are many examples of
intermediate tomb construction; many collective tombs
are constructed in the sloping hillside by cutting a deep
trench, lining it with megalithic slabs, and roofing it with
capstones that are on ground level – the entrance of the
tomb being in the natural slope of the hill. Indeed, in
studying the construction of these intermediate tombs in
south Spain, southern France, and the Paris Basin we may
be given some inkling of how surface megalithic tombs
were constructed. Perhaps a barrow was first constructed
with a deep trench into which the megaliths were slid, the
capstones were then floated over, and the barrow material
heaped over the top.

There is certainly nothing about these 'intermediate'
forms of construction to suggest laziness, or the decay of
the best constructional traditions of megalithic architecture. What we have called the 'sub-megalithic' tombs,
however, are in a different category. The essential constructional peculiarity of these tombs is that the capstone
instead of resting on two orthostats and appearing roughly
level, has one end resting on the ground – the whole monument being triangular in section. For this strange and fairly
rare kind of monument, which exists in western France,
Wales, and Ireland – many names have been suggested,
such as *primary*, *earth-fast*, *demi-dolmen*, or *half-dolmen*.
The term earth-fast seems, perhaps, the most suitable, because it admirably expresses the essential constructional
feature of this type of monument, namely that one end of
the capstone is fast on the ground, and is not there by
accident. Now, quite naturally, many nineteenth-century
antiquaries were puzzled by the earth-fast tomb, some
arguing that it was merely a normal megalithic tomb in a
state of collapse, others insisting that it was not a ruined

37

tomb but one deliberately constructed in this way. The problem is really much the same as the dispute about free-standing tombs and barrows; we cannot prove that all tombs apparently earth-fast at the present day were always so – some of them may well be ruined, normal surface tombs – but it seems very likely that a great number of the earth-fast sites were always like that, and indeed may have had very little covering of barrow over them. This type of megalithic tomb need not detain us long; neither should the other strange type of sub-megalithic tomb which the French call the *demi-allée couverte*. In this type of monument, of which there are a few examples in Finis-tère and perhaps in Ireland, there are no capstones at all, and the side-stones lean inwards to meet at the top in an entirely V-sectioned monument. As far as is known to me this is an extremely rare kind of monument: like the earth-fast chamber it is a makeshift attempt at proper megalithic construction.

We may perhaps now usefully bring this discussion of construction to an end by summarizing it in the form of Table 1.

Type	*Distribution*	*Barrows*
Rock-cut tombs	Restricted	Rare
Surface tombs	Widespread	Normal
Intermediate tombs	Restricted	Rare
Sub-megalithic tombs (earth-fast and *demi-allée couverte*)	Restricted	Very rare

Table 1

This is only a form of shorthand to assist the memory of those who do not specialize in the study of megalithic tombs. So must be our discussion of the form of the chambers and of barrows; it is not possible or useful or wise to try and squeeze the wide variety of construction and form revealed by the collective tombs of western Europe into an over-rigid classificatory scheme. Such schemes, and any conventions of naming which such schemes propose, must be thought of only as conveniences for discussion, in the same way as when we discuss and describe Christian ecclesiastical buildings we speak of rectangular churches and cruciform churches and circular churches. These varieties of form must reflect deliberate schemes in the minds of architects and builders; they may not reflect differences in essential belief or ritual (though, of course, they may), but if we are describing and studying Christian church architecture we must have in our minds first ideas of standard forms and names for them. That is the purpose of any proposed classification of the plans of collective tombs; it is not an end in itself but a way of describing and studying the tombs, and one of the ways by which analysis can move towards the important historical problems that we are trying to solve as archaeologists when we study these monuments: who were the builders, whence did they come, how and where did they live, why did they spread over western Europe, and what contributions, if any, did they make to the future heritage of prehistoric Europe?'

One of the very earliest classifications of the form of prehistoric burial chambers was that attempted by the Reverend W. C. Lukis in 1864. Lukis was extremely interested in megaliths; he travelled widely in Europe as well as the British Isles studying them and indeed produced in 1875 a guide to the principal chambered barrows of the Morbihan. He proposed to distinguish at first between two basic types of prehistoric burial chamber:

1. simple chambers, which included all chambers formed by a single roofing stone supported by two or more orthostats; and

2. complex chambers, which were chambers with passages (or, as Lukis called them 'covered ways') leading to them.

In this first essay at classification Lukis did not seem to have found a place for a type of monument which is very common in western Europe, the long parallel-sided monument with no passage leading to it. The Swedish archaeologist, Oscar Montelius, improved on Lukis's classification by including this type. Montelius's classification was first propounded in 1876 and continued as follows:

1. simple chambers consisting of a single roofing stone supported by two or more side stones;
2. rectangular or polygonal chambers approached by a passage; and
3. elongated rectangular chambers with no passages.

To the first class Montelius gave the Swedish name *dös*, pl. *dösar* (or the Danish equivalent *dysse* and *dysser*) and this was translated into English by archaeologists as 'dolmen', a word we will have something to say about soon. For his second class Montelius proposed the Swedish names *grafvar med gång* and *gånggrift*, and the terms 'passage grave' in England and '*dolmen à galerie*' in France are generally used as equivalents for these names. Montelius called his third class *hällkistor*, which is generally translated as long stone cists. This term 'long stone cist' is not a very fortunate English translation; it is confusing on account of its ready association in the mind with the small stone cists characteristic of many periods of the Early Bronze Age, and which differ from the megalithic tombs in size, in the fact that they are usually underground, and also usually individual graves. In France the term *allée couverte* (or 'covered gallery') is used for what Montelius meant by *hällkistor*, and in English the phrase 'gallery grave' is now generally used for this type of tomb.

This classification of Montelius needs some modification and elaboration to make it fit the increased knowledge we have at the present day of prehistoric collective tombs. His first class should not be defined in terms of a single roofing stone but in terms of the smallness of the chamber. This first class is essentially a small chamber – round, rectangular, or polygonal in form unapproached by any passage. It is proposed to describe these tombs here as 'simple

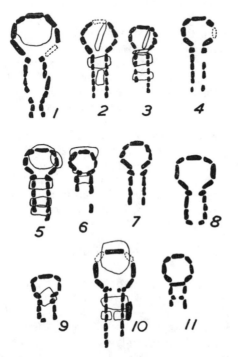

Fig. 5 – Megalithic passage graves from Portugal. (1) Ordem. (2–11) Pavia. (*After Vergilio Correia*)

chambers', or 'single chambers', and to revive Lukis's old term (e.g. the typical 'rectangular simple chambers' from Denmark, Fig. 7, p. 48). It is also proposed that for convenience of reference we should refer to 'round single chambers', 'polygonal single chambers', and 'rectangular single chambers'. When, fifteen years ago, the present writer first proposed a modification of the Lukis–Montelian system which recognized the morphological variety that exists within each category, he proposed the terms A-Dolmen and B-Dolmen for what is now suggested should be described as 'single rectangular' and 'single polygonal chambers', but these terms were never widely used, and it seems now that any phrase in English using the word 'dolmen' ought to be avoided if possible.

The typical passage grave really looks like the round single chamber or the polygonal single chamber with a passage leading to it. It consists then of two distinct parts, the passage or approaching element leading from the edge of the barrow which was not normally used for burial, and the chamber itself where the burials took place, which is usually wider and bigger than and clearly demarcated from the passage. There are several good examples of passage graves illustrated by plans here (see Figs 5, p. 41, and 17, p. 101) and this is the normal or classic type widespread in western Europe. The main areas of distribution of passage graves are southern Spain, Portugal, north-western France, west Wales, Ireland, and Scotland; there are also passage graves in north-eastern Spain and southern France, and in Sardinia. The Sicilian rock-cut tombs are also mainly passage graves.

In some tombs which are of the passage grave type there is no sharp break in the walls of the tomb – the distinction in form between passage and chamber has broken down. This type of passage grave is worth distinguishing on formal grounds from the classic passage grave (or Pavian passage grave, as I have elsewhere called it), and a convenient label for it is the Undifferentiated or V-shaped passage grave. This type of monument occurs in southern Spain, in Brittany, the Channel Islands, and in the Isles of Scilly, and in one or two of these localities the passage graves are very small and the side-walls nearer parallel than V-shaped. For these rather specialized versions of the undifferentiated passage grave Dr Hugh Hencken suggested the name 'entrance grave', and it is a very useful name for

42

these small tombs in the Isles of Scilly, Finistère, and County Waterford.

The third of Montelius's classes, the gallery graves, can also usefully be split into two, the normal or classic gallery graves (which I have elsewhere called the Loire galleries)

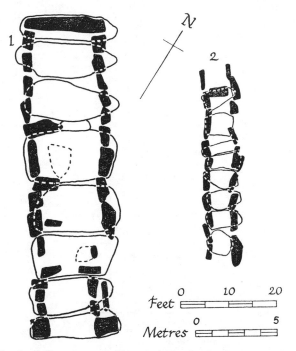

Fig. 6 – Gallery graves in France. (1) Essé (*after L'Helgouach*) (2) Tressé (*after Collum*)

(Fig. 6), and the wedge-shaped galleries. The wedge-shaped galleries can be seen from those illustrated in Fig. 22 (p. 120) from Ireland and north-western France. They are really the reverse of the undifferentiated passage grave, and get narrower from the entrance towards the end.

The barrows associated with these types vary considerably, but certain generalizations of a useful kind can be made. These refer, of course, to the surface tombs. Here it is fair to say that the majority of the round single chambers, polygonal single chambers, and passage graves are normally associated with round barrows, while ovate, long and rectangular barrows are more commonly found with rectangular single chambers and gallery graves. The seven types into which we have split Montelius's classification can now be summarized in Table 2.

	Type	*Distribution*	*Barrow*
Single chambers	1. Single round chambers	Restricted	Round
	2. Single polygonal chambers	Same as 4	Round
	3. Single rectangular chambers	Same as 6	Long
Passage graves	4. Passage graves (normal or Pavian)	Widespread	Round
	5. Undifferentiated passage graves (V-shaped and entrance graves)	Restricted	Round
Gallery graves	6. Gallery graves (normal or Loire)	Widespread	Long
	7. Wedge-gallery graves	Restricted	Long

Table 2 – Types of plan of megalithic tombs in western Europe

It is worth emphasizing that this sevenfold classification of types is to facilitate description and analysis of the thousands of tombs that exist in western Europe, and that many of the labels used, like 'single' or 'passage', are used in a formal nomenclatural sense only; it does not mean that the single tombs must be necessarily earlier or later or more widespread or less rich than the others – and the addition of a passage to a tomb formally of types 6 and 7 does not turn it into a passage grave. Obviously these forms merge into each other; indeed they must if we are going to argue, as many do, that some types developed out of each other; obviously, too, for morphological description, one must be sure of dealing with a complete tomb – passage graves that have lost their passages through the ravages of road-menders, builders, and farmers will look like types 1, 2, or 3. Then again, it is important to remember that this classification deals only with the main varieties of tombs found in western Europe – the standard and widespread varieties. Every area in which megalithic architecture flourished produced its own regional versions of the basic plans of tombs, and these not only defy classification, but no useful purpose is served by such attempts. It is only an academic exercise to argue whether for example some of the very remarkable tombs in Ireland and the Orkneys and Shetlands are gallery graves or passage graves. We must rather think of the form of megalithic tombs in terms of the spread of styles of funerary architecture, with certain basic patterns on which regional and local variations were made.

Burial chambers may have side-chambers opening out of them or out of their passages; and chambers may be divided up into a number of smaller chambers, this division being done by transverse elements or *septae*. This segmentation or septalization may be done by jambs projecting from each side, or by transverse stones or septal stones, or by a combination of projecting jambs and transverse stones. Septal stones sometimes reach, say, half-way up the height of a chamber; at other times they reach to the roof and are perforated with a hole large enough to admit the passage of a body. These holes, which may be round or square, can also be constructed of two touching projecting stones with hollowed-out adjoining edges. To these holes

45

the name 'portholes' has been given, for obvious reasons. Portholes occur in southern Iberia and in a small number of tombs in France and Britain, as well as in the gallery graves of southern Sweden. Tomb No. 20 at Los Millares in south-eastern Spain (plan in Fig. 8, p. 63) shows side-chambers, septal slabs, and several portholes.

One point of importance is worth stressing here. Many burial chambers appear at the present day quite easy to get into; one just walks straight in from the surrounding countryside. It must not be thought that, when these tombs were originally built and used, access was equally easy. There would be the necessity of clearing away the closing and blocking deposits to which we have referred, which would be filling the forecourt and entrance to the chamber or passage. In other burial chambers the orthostats are so arranged that it would not be possible to get into the chamber merely by removing blocking and closing deposits; it would be necessary to remove an orthostat, and it is unlikely (and in most cases constructionally impossible) that this could be done. We must therefore distinguish between *open* and *closed* burial chambers; and note that sometimes it is a portion of a burial chamber – like the last segment of a segmented gallery grave – which is so closed. Access to closed chambers sometimes could be, and was, obtained by moving a capstone. But whether burial chambers were formally closed or open, in the terms of these definitions we are adopting, they were almost always hidden from view. It is the method of access to the tomb, not its general appearance, that is signified by the words open and closed.

There are two words widely met with in megalithic architecture which it is not proposed here to use in exact senses when discussing the megalithic tombs of western Europe. These are *tholos* and *dolmen*. The term chamber tomb is one very well known and used in the archaeology of Greece and the Aegean islands, and there the terms *tholos* and *dromos* are used to describe the chamber and the approaching passage of a beehive-shaped tomb, like,

The Prehistoric Collective Tombs

for example, the famous Treasury of Atreus at Mycenae, or the tomb on the island of Euboea. The dome or *tholos* of such tombs, and the approach or *dromos* correspond, of course, formally and functionally to the chamber and passage of the passage graves we have been describing; it is quite reasonable to refer to the west European passage graves (or at least those that are dry-walled and roofed by corbelling) as *tholoi*, and equally reasonable to call the Mycenaen, Cretan, and other *tholoi*, passage graves. Personally, it seems to me more convenient to restrict the terms *tholos* and *dromos* to descriptions of the Greek tombs, but to use a different terminology for the west European monuments, and not to have any terminology for western European monuments which overemphasizes perhaps the distinction between whether a passage grave is rock-cut, roofed with orthostats, or roofed by corbelling. But readers should bear in mind that the word *tholos* is used by some writers in describing certain tombs in western Europe and that when they do so they almost always mean a corbelled passage grave such as New Grange or Île Longue or the tombs in the Alcalá cemetery of southern Portugal.

The word 'dolmen' is perhaps the most widespread in megalithic literature. It occurs in archaeological literature in the late eighteenth century as a general descriptive term for megalithic tombs, and as such is still used in France where one talks of the 'dolmens' of a region or department and asks the way to a 'dolmen' in the sense of any megalithic monument. At the present day in English literature the word is used either for a very ruined monument whose original form might have been anything (that is to say for an indeterminate megalithic structure) or is equated with the words *dysee* or *dös* of the Montelian classification (and it is in this sense that we talk of the 'Dolmen Period' of northern European archaeology and our German colleagues of the *Dolmenzeit* – the time when single polygonal and rectangular chambers belonging to Montelius's *dysse* class were being made). Neither usage is very helpful, and the existence of the two usages together with a quite different usage in France, where, as we have said, not only are all megalithic monuments referred to as dolmens, but passage graves are called *'dolmens à galerie'*, makes the term one which is perhaps better omitted from any modern attempt at exact description. In Ireland a particular form of chamber tomb is often described as a 'portal dolmen'; and they also occur in western Britain. These are interesting monuments which, like so many chamber tombs, do not fit exactly into the sevenfold classifications suggested above. They are really something between a single rectangular

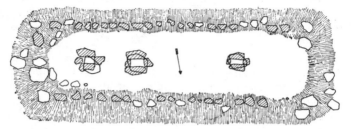

Fig. 7 – Long *dysse* with three chambers, Denmark

chamber and a small gallery grave. 'Portal dolmen' will do as a phrase among those for whom the word dolmen has no fears and implications; otherwise such monuments as those figured ought to be described non-committally as 'single rectangular chambers with portals'.

Hitherto we have assumed that we are correct in describing these structures, whose method of building and external form we have been discussing, as tombs. Antiquaries argued for decades over their real purpose, and were, of course, confused by the appearance of free-standing monuments, by the existence of cup-marks and grooves on some of the stones, by little exact evidence from excavation and comparative archaeology, and by the glamour of the Druids as they appeared in the writings of classical authors. It was suggested that the chamber tombs were houses, astronomical observatories, places of augury, seats of justice, temples, altars, oratories. The following passage from an unpublished book of the late eighteenth century, written by a Chancellor of Bangor Cathedral, gives a typical and vivid account of the extraordinary ceremonies which were alleged to have taken place on the tops of burial chambers:[1]

> The Druids enterprised nothing nor entered upon any Great important Action, without Augury, Aruspicy and Divination. The Cromllech or Inclined Plane was notably well fitted for the Opening, Extensio.. and Examination of the Entrails of any kind of victims; and its gradual Slope was very favourable to the descent of the flowing blood, as well as Other Liquids, a victim laid in such a position Could be better Observed by both the Priests and People; and all the several Convulsive Agitations of the heart, Intestines, in the agonies of Death, be better seen, than either in an upright or horizontal one.[2]

Excavations in the second half of the nineteenth century revealed the true original purpose of these megalithic chambers, and the sepulchral purpose of the tombs needs no further arguing at the present day.

The customary funerary rite practised is burial; and the excavation of chamber tombs usually produces unburnt skeletons. Inhumation, generally in the contracted position, is the usual rite, but cremation is reported from some tombs in Spain and France and well-attested in Irish chamber tombs. Sometimes there are very few skeletons in a chamber tomb; at others the number is very large indeed. The tomb of St Eugène near Carcassonne in southern France had contained three hundred corpses; tombs have been found in Denmark and Sweden containing about a hundred skeletons; in England and Wales the greatest

1. It should be explained that in Wales the word *cromlech* is used much as *dolmen* is used in France; a general term for all megalithic tombs. In France, confusingly, cromlech means a stone circle.

2. Richard Farrington, *Snowdonia Druidica or the Druid Monuments of Snowdon* (MS. in the National Library of Wales, Aberystwyth, dated 1769, pp. 42–3).

number of skeletons found was at Pant y Saer in Anglesey where there were fifty-four. Where there are many individuals buried in a chamber tomb it is often found that while one or two skeletons are intact, most of the others are broken or have bones missing. Archaeologists, in their excavation reports on chamber tombs, have often referred to the chaotic disorder of the majority of the bones; sometimes it looks as though some attempt at tidying took place – a passage grave at Trolhöj in Zealand (Denmark) revealed that many of the crania of the skeletons had been collected in heaps by the wall of the chamber. Some chamber tombs contain small cists or walls protecting some of the burials. Rosenberg's researches in Danish chambered tombs have shown that sometimes contents of the tomb were moved out into the forecourt.

The main features of burial ritual in west European chamber tombs that require explanation are the following : the large number of individuals represented in many of the tombs (sometimes there are more skeletons in a chamber than it could have held bodies if they were all put there together soon after death and at the same time); the disordered, fragmentary, and fractional condition of the majority of the skeletons; and that a few skeletons in the chambers are sometimes ordered, unbroken, and complete while the others are disordered, fragmentary, and fractional. Some tombs are rich in grave-goods – pottery, cult objects, arrowheads, weapons, and tools, and there is often evidence of complicated rituals in chamber and forecourt with traces of fire. Animal bones occur in the burials – joints of meat laid with the dead, or remains of funeral feasts.

Many interpretations of these archaeological facts have been put forward. One suggests that the tombs were the tombs of chieftains, represented by the intact bodies, while the disordered bodies around represent the followers and wives slain at the funeral to accompany their lord to the other world. There is little doubt that some chamber tombs – the finest Mycenaen *tholoi* perhaps – were designed for

The Prehistoric Collective Tombs

a chief and perhaps his wife; and there is good evidence for *sati* or *suttee* in early historical times in Europe.[1] Some archaeologists believe most chamber tombs to be those of chieftains. Others believe the tombs to be communal ossuaries, to which the bodies were moved, after the flesh had perished, from other temporary resting-places. The majority of archaeologists at the present day, however, believe that most chamber tombs were collective tombs, used over a period of time – often perhaps a long period of time – by a family or group of people. Keiller and Piggott claim that the evidence of the chamber at Lanhill North in Wiltshire allows of only one interpretation, and that is the successive collective use of the tomb by a family group over a period of years.

The evidence of west European chamber tombs enables us to build up some kind of picture of the burial ritual involved. The chamber tombs of Greece and the Aegean have been studied in much greater detail and, of course, provide much more detailed information. Recently, Professor G. E. Mylonas summarized his interpretation of the Mycenaean archaeological evidence as follows :

The dead, perhaps on a wooden bier, decked in his clothes and ornaments, surrounded by his belongings and well provided with supplies to speed him on his way to the unknown, was left on the floor of the chamber tomb . . . then the door was walled up, a libation or toast offered in his honour by each participant in the burial perhaps accompanied by the calling of his name, the dromos was filled in, a funeral feast was held, and a marker was placed to indicate the position of the grave. When a second death occurred in the family, the dromos was cleared, the packing of the door was removed, the chamber was made ready and fumigated, and if the body of the first tenant had not entirely decayed, burned offerings were made to propitiate its spirit and keep it in the grave. The second body was then laid in state on the

1. For a tenth-century account see *Antiquity*, 1934, pp. 58 ff.

floor . . . burial succeeded burial until the floor-space was occupied and the bodies were decomposed. Then room was made for the latest addition by packing the bones of the ancestors in cists, by sweeping them up against the sides of the grave, or even by throwing them out into the dromos.[1]

What, Professor Mylonas asks, does all this mean in terms of belief? He suggests, tentatively, that it means:

the spirit of the departed was sentient and was around the grave as long as the flesh was in existence; the corpse was treated with respect; it had to be provided with supplies; it had to be given favourite objects that in life belonged to it; it had to be kept in the grave by walled doors. The moment the body was dissolved and was transformed into a pile of bones, it no longer had need of anything; there was no danger that its spirit would reappear; the spirit had descended into its final abode never to return; the bones could be swept aside or even thrown out.

It is not suggested here, by quoting this passage *in extenso*, that the collective tombs of western Europe were built by Mycenaeans – although this view has been advanced. Nor is it suggested that the picture derived from Greek excavation is applicable in all its detail to western Europe and that we can postulate among our forebears in Iberia, France, and the British Isles the Homeric ideas of Psyche and Hades. It is merely suggested that Mylonas's summary of the customs of the Greek chamber-tomb builders, and the meaning of the customs practised by the people who buried their dead in these tombs, forms a very good working hypothesis as to the notions that *may* have lain behind the burial customs of our western European tomb builders.

We cannot evaluate the justice of this comparison until

1. This and the succeeding extract are from Mylonas's paper on Homeric and Mycenaean Burial Customs in the *American Journal of Archaeology*, 1949, pp. 56 ff.

we have accumulated more facts about the chamber tombs of western Europe themselves. Were the east Mediterranean chamber tombs anything to do with the western European chamber tombs, or did the megalithic chamber tombs originate in Iberia or in the British Isles or in Denmark? We now have some idea of how they were built and the forms they took. We must now turn to the Iberian and the north European megaliths because they, between them, really provide the clues to our problems about the origins of these chamber tombs. The British, Irish, and French tombs can be understood and explained only after we have adopted some working hypothesis about the Iberian and Scandinavian megaliths. Both Iberian and Scandinavian megaliths have been hotly disputed about for nearly a hundred years. Let us now plunge into these disputes!

3

NORTHERN EUROPE AND IBERIA

MEGALITHIC tombs occur in northern Europe in the following areas: in Denmark, in Sweden south of a line from Oslo to Stockholm, in northern Germany and northern Holland. In Denmark the megalithic tombs occur chiefly on the east coast of Jutland from Randers to Flensburg, and on the islands of the sound – they are very common in Zealand, Falster, Laaland, Langeland, and Fyen, and it has been estimated that nearly 3,500 megalithic tombs survive on these islands. In Germany the megalithic tombs are found north of a line from Hanover through Magdeburg to Berlin, in Schleswig-Holstein, Hanover, and Mecklenburg, north Saxony and Brandenburg, and extend westwards into west Hanover, Oldenburg, and northern Westphalia, and into northern Holland (into the Dutch provinces of Drenthe and Groningen), as well as eastwards beyond the Oder into Pomerania. It is perhaps worth emphasizing here that there is not much distributional continuity between the megalithic tombs of France and those of the Scandinavian–north German area. Belgium, south Holland, and south-west Germany have very few burial chambers.

We have already mentioned Montelius's scheme of classification of the Scandinavian megalithic tombs which distinguished *dös*, *gånggrift*, and *hällkistor* and are generally translated into English as 'dolmen', 'passage grave', and 'stone cist'. Montelius was really elaborating, in the last quarter of the nineteenth century, the earlier classifications current in northern Europe. J. J. Worsaae in Denmark, much earlier, had distinguished two groups, the *Stendysser* and the *Jaettestüer* ('giants' chambers' or 'tombs') or *Gangbygningen* ('passage buildings'). The *Stendysser* (our equiva-

54

lent transliteration was dolmen) were single chambers in long or round barrows, and Worsaae distinguished, as Danish folk and archaeological nomenclature does at the present day, between the *Langdysser* (single chambers in long barrows) and the *Runddysser* (single chambers in round barrows). A. P. Madsen, in his *Antiquités préhistoriques du Danemark* in 1869, had the same scheme, and it was introduced into England by Lord Avebury (then Sir John Lubbock) in his *Prehistoric Times* and by James Fergusson in his *Rude Stone Monuments*.

Montelius later elaborated his scheme, recognizing no less than nine forms of megalithic tomb belonging to the Scandinavian stone age; we need not go into all this detail here. What does concern us is that the Montelian system in its basic threefold essentials was widely used as a classification of megalithic tombs all over western Europe, and that he saw his scheme not merely as a classificatory one but also as one of evolutionary sequence; that is to say, it was in his mind not merely a taxonomic system, but a typological sequence. He argued that the *dösar*, *dysser*, or 'dolmens' evolved into the passage grave in Scandinavia, and then that the passage grave developed into the long stone cist. Montelius also evolved a system of dividing the Northern Stone Age into four periods based on the typology of stone axes as well as of stone tombs. These periods were as follows :

Period	Axes	Tombs
I	Pointed-Butted	None
II	Thin-Butted	Dösar/Dysser
III	Thick-Butted	Passage Graves
IV	Flint Daggers	Long Stone Cists

This scheme is still used as a classificatory basis for the Stone Age in northern Europe. In the wall charts and labels in the National Museum at Copenhagen at the moment the Neolithic is divided into a Dolmen Period from 2500 to 2300 B.C., a Passage-Grave Period from 2300 to 1800 B.C.,

and a Flint Dagger/Stone Cist Period from 1800 to 1500
B.C. Montelius's Period I has disappeared, and the axe with
pointed butt is regarded as the final derivative of a Mesolithic axe.

This classic idea of the evolution of the megalithic tombs
in northern Europe is still widely held, and as it seems to
explain the origin of all the types of tomb found in western
Europe, we must pay some more attention to it. After all,
if it is really right, it answers all our questions about the
origin, development, and diffusion of megalithic tombs.
The dolmen builders of Montelius's Northern Period II are
described as agriculturists cultivating emmer, bread wheat,
and barley and keeping cattle, sheep, and pigs; their pottery has three characteristic forms, namely collared flasks,
funnel-necked beakers, and amphorae. As we have said,
Montelius thought these people originated in Scandinavia,
and the *dös/dysse* form of great stone tomb just started –
as indeed inventions in material culture have to start somewhere and some time. Other archaeologists have been in-
creasingly unhappy about this idea; some have argued that
these stone tombs were introduced by settlers from the
west and have pointed to the occurrence of 'dolmens' in
western Europe. As we have seen, the word 'dolmen' is a
very inexact term, but it is true that we can find in many
parts of western Europe single rectangular and polygonal
megalithic chambers. Nevertheless there are very few
monuments in western Europe precisely like the *langdysser*
and *runddysser* of Denmark.

At one time it seemed to myself and others that the Scandinavian *dös/dysse* type of tomb could be explained as
degenerate developments of the northern European passage
graves in much the same way as, we shall see, Fleure and
Forde argued in explanation of the 'dolmens' of Iberia. It
is true that in northern Europe many of the tombs formally
classified as of the *dös/dysse* type must on account of their
grave-goods be dated to Montelius's Period III or even IV.
In Sweden, no monument put in Period II by its form has
actually yielded material grave-goods of this period. But

many of the *dös/dysse* type in Denmark do yield Period II material; and the place of the collared flasks, funnel-necked beakers, and amphorae has been established stratigraphically as earlier than Period III material and tombs.

What is even more important is that this pottery occurs in Denmark and Schleswig-Holstein in earth-graves, i.e. in non-megalithic tombs, and similar earth-graves with similar pottery are found in eastern Germany and Poland right to the Upper Vistula. As Gordon Childe argued in his *Dawn of European Civilization* (1957) the culture represented in many of the *dös/dysee* tombs – a culture of pottery, agriculture, polygonal battle-axes, and amber beads – is 'one specialized facies of a wider cultural continuum'.

Our problem has been taken one stage further towards its contemporary solution by the work of men like Becker and Troels-Smith on the Danish Neolithic. Professor C. J. Becker has made a special study of the Danish Neolithic pottery; and in order to avoid confusion with the Montelian terminology based mainly on tombs and axes, he has followed Jazdzewski's example of calling the first Neolithic culture of Denmark the 'Funnel-Beaker Culture', and has abandoned Montelius's terms, using instead the phrases 'Danish Early Neolithic' (equals Montelius II, or I/II, i.e. the *dös/dysse* period), 'Danish Middle Neolithic (Montelius III, the passage grave period), and 'Danish Late Neolithic' (Montelius IV, the dagger/stone cist period). He has further divided the Early Neolithic into three periods, A, B, and C, based on the typology of funnel-beakers and stratigraphy; and he shows that this Early Neolithic culture is only associated with *dös/dysse* tombs in Period C, and then only in certain groups of his Period C. Becker in his Period C distinguishes a North Jutland Group, a South Danish Group, and a Bornholm–South Swedish Group, and it is the South Danish Group only which has *dös/dysse* tombs. To quote Becker's own conclusions on this matter, 'the dolmen in Denmark makes its first appearance in the South Danish C Group . . . what hitherto has been regarded as the earliest type – a narrow rectangular chamber built of side-stones of equal height – really seems to be earlier than other forms'.

We have, at least in this matter, swung back to Montelius's view. It now looks as though we should regard the 'dolmens' of northern Europe not as derived from western Europe nor as degenerate passage graves (though I still think the polygonal *dös/dysse* type in round barrows are intimately connected with the passage graves) but as independent inventions in northern Europe – a translation into megalithic architecture of the cist that occurred in the more widespread earth-graves. This translation began on Zealand, and later the 'dolmen' form spread all over Denmark and northern Germany. It is worth emphasizing that tombs of the *dös/dysse* type of northern Europe are not collective tombs in the sense of the western European collective tomb; they often contain no more than six skeletons, sometimes only one or two, and moreover they are sometimes quite small – for example six feet long by two feet wide.

When did this spontaneous generation of megalithic tombs in south Denmark take place? Childe has argued that Montelius's Period II (Becker's Early Neolithic) cannot be earlier than the end of the Danubian Period II, and would date it 2100 to 1900 B.C. The Danish National Museum and much of official Danish archaeological literature would put the period earlier, beginning at 2500 B.C. and ending at 2300 or 2200 B.C. Our dating really depends to a large extent on the interpretation of the Middle Neolithic in Scandinavia, and on our views on the development and origin of passage graves, to which we now turn. This period has been divided on the basis of pottery styles (into the details of which we need not now go) into four periods, a, b, c, and d. From the beginning of it there were passage graves; and the earliest passage graves occur in northern Jutland, the islands, and areas like Sylt. The question is, do they represent a local development in northern Europe, as at first Montelius thought, or do they represent a spread to northern Europe of the people who built passage graves in

Northern Europe and Iberia

France and Iberia? There is no doubt that one can build up a typological sequence between selected *dös/dysse* monuments and the passage graves, but it is not very easy; and we must emphasize that the *dös/dysse* monuments were not collective tombs, whereas the passage graves are large communal vaults containing often as many as a hundred skeletons. There is equally no doubt that exact morphological parallels can be found between the northern European passage graves and those of western Europe, but this does not imply that the western European passage graves are the ancestors of the northern European passage graves. The reverse might be the case; and it has been argued, and can well be argued, that the origin of our western European passage graves lies in a movement from Denmark and Sweden, by people who had developed the passage grave out of the *dös/dysse* which they had themselves invented. Here, then, we see the megalith builders as the Vikings of 2000 B.C., setting forth to the British Isles and France, and on to Iberia and the west Mediterranean.

All these views have been canvassed; it seems to me that the most probable view at present, as well as the most widely held, is that while the *dös/dysse* type of monument originated in south Denmark in Period II C, the passage grave builders who arrrived in Period III A came by sea from western Europe. The questions are then, Whence?, How?, Why?, and When? The precise area is difficult to define; I would myself think in terms of direct contact with Brittany and Portugal, and that the route taken was via the English Channel. Others have argued for the spread to have taken place round the north of Scotland, claiming a likeness between some of the north Scottish tomb plans and the T-shaped passage graves of northern Europe.

At Bygholm, near Horsens in Jutland, there was found a hoard dating from the beginning of the passage grave period. It consisted of four flat axes of copper, three spiral armlets, and a copper dagger, with a midrib on one face. This dagger is very like those from passage graves in southern Portugal and could perhaps be used to establish a synchronism between the early passage graves of northern Europe and Iberia. In the last phase of the Danish Middle Neolithic (Period III), pottery is often found decorated with face or *oculi* motifs; and similar motifs are found on idols and on pottery in Iberia (the *symbolkeramik* of the Leisners, which we shall soon be discussing) and on the walls of some tombs in Iberia and France. It certainly looks as though contacts were maintained through the Middle Neolithic period of Denmark between western Europe and the north.

Our absolute dating in the north must depend to a certain extent on our absolute dating of the passage graves in western Europe; but, fortunately, we have other evidence which both gives us an independent chronology of the northern European passage graves, but also if their western derivation is correct, gives us fresh and independent evidence for the date of the French and Iberian collective tombs. It has been shown that the arrival of bell beakers in northern Europe falls in the latter half of the passage grave period; the synchronism of beakers is with Middle Neolithic C. Imports of a type belonging to the Aunjetitz Early Bronze Age culture of central Europe found in Middle Neolithic D contexts show that some passage graves lasted through to after 1650. It is difficult to disagree with those who would date the Danish Middle Neolithic from 2000 B.C., or even before, to 1600 B.C.; and the *floruit* of the passage graves of northern Europe is approximately the first half of the second millennium B.C. If we ask what other elements of material culture these western settlers brought, the answer must be practically nothing, because the *oculi*-ornamented pottery dates from a late phase in their development in northern Europe. When Professor Christopher Hawkes (following C. A. Nordman) was arguing for the western origin of the northern European tombs of *dös/dysse* type, he said that the northern dolmen was due to a 'conversion to the megalithic religion, by which is meant the acceptance in the coastlands of Denmark and north Germany . . . of the magic power of the religion brought by the Atlantic voyagers'.[1] Now that it seems likely that the *dös/dysse* type of monument was independently developed in northern Europe, we can perhaps see the passage grave builders, instead, as the Atlantic voyagers who effected the conversion to a new religion, or at least to new mortuary cults; and see this conversion as all the more easily effected in an area where already small megalithic tombs, the *dös/dysse* type, were being constructed.

Once the tradition of passage grave building and the use of collective tombs was established in northern Europe it flourished exceedingly; and some very remarkable local versions of the passage grave were invented, notably the T-shaped passage grave. Was it the elaboration of the T-shaped passage grave and the gradual reduction in the size of the passage that ultimately produced the long stone cist or the gallery grave of Montelius Period IV, the Danish Late Neolithic? Montelius certainly argued this, and it is likely that this evolutionary sequence is responsible for some at least of the galleries of the Late Neolithic. But some of the Swedish and German gallery graves are, at least superficially, very like the gallery graves of the Paris Basin : they are sunk in the ground, have porthole partitions, and even contain some of the coarse flat-bottomed pots that are common in the Paris Basin gallery graves and in various 'secondary Neolithic' contexts in France. It looks as though there may have been, in the Late Neolithic period in northern Europe, a fresh incursion of megalith builders from the west, and, apparently, from the Paris Basin. Most archaeologists, perhaps rather reluctantly, have accepted this point of view, some suggesting the contacts were by land across Belgium and Westphalia to south Sweden, others that they were directly by sea from France. From the archaeological material found in the Danish Late Neolithic it would seem likely, on the basis of central European contacts, that the gallery graves of northern Europe dated from between 1600 and 1400 B.C.

1. C. F. C. Hawkes, *The Prehistoric Foundations of Europe to the Mycenean Age*, 1940, p. 211.

The Megalith Builders of Western Europe

reason
for
Cont
erson

We have engaged on this brief summary of the problems
and controversies surrounding megalithic monuments in
northern Europe because a discussion of them seems to
lead to three conclusions. The first is that megalithic origins
may well be complicated and multiple, even in one limited
European area. Secondly, if, as we have argued, the Danish
dysser were being built in Early Neolithic C, and the port-
holed Swedish gallery graves between 1600 and 1400 B.C.,
megalithic tomb construction in northern Europe lasted
for perhaps eight hundred years at least: we cannot, then,
usefully talk of a 'megalithic period' in Europe. But the
third lesson seems to be this: the passage grave builders
who arrived in the north from western Europe appear (at
least from the archaeological evidence, and that is all we
have) to have brought with them no more than skill in
tomb building and such religious and military power and
prestige as would compel the aborigines among whom they
settled to great architectural labours.

With these three lessons in mind we now move to Iberia,
another classic area, for the study of megalithic problems
and controversies. The Iberian peninsula is very rich in
chamber tombs, and the most striking feature of this distribution is the absence of chamber tombs from eastern and
central Spain. The areas in which the chamber tombs occur
form a wide strip on the north-east, west, and south sides
of the peninsula. Distributionally these tombs fall into two
groups, a main one south and west of a line from Oviedo
through Salamanca and Cordoba to Alicante, and a smaller
group in the north-east, in the Basque provinces and those
of Catalonia, Navarre, and Aragon. The two groups are
almost quite separate from each other, and the north-east
group is geographically and culturally connected with the
south French megaliths. We will discuss the main south
and west group first.

Los Millares, in Almeria, is a cemetery of seventy-five
chamber tombs immediately outside a walled township of
the same date and culture; it lies a few miles up the river
Andarax from the modern city of Almeria. Almizaraque is

an extremely fine corbelled passage grave not far from the sea with a village near by. In the province of Granada there are many famous groups of tombs, notably Gor, Los Eriales, and Montefrio. In Malaga province at Antequera are the three fine passage graves we have already mentioned, set in modified natural hillocks – the Cuevas de Viera, Romeral, and de Menga; and near by a group of rock-cut tombs at Alcaide. The chamber tombs of Seville province occur first along the Guadalquivir river – notably the Cueva de la Pastora, the Dolmen de Matarrubilla, and

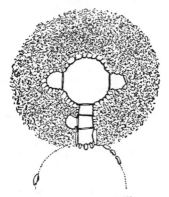

Fig. 8 – Plan of Los Millares
Tomb 20 (*after the Sirets*)

the group at Gandul, and then spread up into the foothills of the Sierra Morena; and it is here in the Sierra Morena that the Cordoban chamber tombs are to be found. Huelva province has some very fine chamber tombs, like de Soto, St Bartolomé, and the El Pozuelo cemetery, and these tombs join on with the Portuguese tombs.

Chamber tombs are very widespread in Portugal and in Galicia. Among the most famous are the cemetery of passage graves at Alcalá in the Algarve, the rock-cut tombs near Lisbon (at Alapraia and Carenque between Lisbon and Estoril) and at Palmella, south of the Tagus, and the great cemetery of passage graves at Pavia. The Gangas de Onis

63

site near Oviedo in north-western Spain has achieved special notoriety among students of archaeology because it is incorporated in a Christian church, a distinction it shares with the megalithic tomb incorporated in the Chapelle des Sept Saints between Guingamp and Lannion in north Brittany.

We have already indicated the distribution of rock-cut passage graves in Iberia; the corbelled dry-walled passage graves (which some would describe as *tholoi*) occur in the south coastal belt from Los Millares to Alcalá. Truly megalithic passage graves occur mainly in the western part of

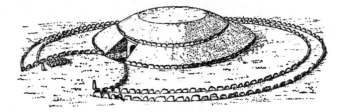

Fig. 9 – Reconstruction of a Millaran tomb by G. and V. Leisner

this belt and in central and northern Portugal; there are also many megalithic passage graves in eastern Granada where a speciality seems to have been made of rectangular and V-shaped chambers. The Huelva–Seville area specialized in all sorts of intermediate constructional devices – not merely the Antequera tombs we have described as constructionally intermediate between rock-cut and surface tombs, but tombs which are constructionally intermediate between megalithic and dry-walled tombs, e.g. the great Matarrubilla tomb which is entirely walled by dry-walling but roofed with capstones. In southern Spain and south Portugal there is very great variety in the plan, as in the construction of the chamber tombs, but the most common plan is the passage grave with a round or polygonal chamber. Side-chambers occur quite commonly at Los Millares and at other sites like Alcalá and Cueva de la Pastora. Portholes and septal slabs seem confined to Los Millares, Almizaraque, and to the rock-cut tombs of the Lisbon area.

Among the tomb plans the most interesting variants, or the most deviationist forms, occur in the south-western Spanish areas – the provinces of Huelva and Seville and Malaga; here we get fine examples of the way in which the passage grave builders varied their traditional widely spread standard plan. One tomb may be extremely long, others develop into bottle-shaped or V-shaped passage graves, while a tomb like the Tumba de la Casilla (Gandul D) in Seville Province could in isolation in France easily be classified as a gallery grave. Indeed, the great variety of tomb types in southern Spain emphasizes that the classification and naming of megalithic types is a convenience for reference and description rather than recognition of absolute types and species. In a recent interesting analysis of archaeological method and typology MacWhite has said that 'megalithic tombs . . . have been the subjects of complicated typologies in which it is difficult to distinguish between differentiations which are observer-imposed and those which are real or inherent in the material itself';[1] and Childe has complained that 'the attribution of a tomb to one or other group is often a matter of taste'.[2] Archaeological description must be to a large extent subjective, but in the present state of our nomenclature there is no other way of describing the megalithic tombs of Seville and Huelva except by saying that they include passage graves, also tombs that by themselves would be classified as gallery graves, and thirdly, monuments varying in type between these two.

Single chambers occur in two areas in the south-west Iberian megalithic province. There are single circular drywalled and orthostat-walled chambers in the Almerian area and single polygonal megalithic chambers in central and northern Portugal.

Single rectangular chambers are very rare in the south-

1. E. MacWhite, *American Anthropologist*, 1956, p. 12.
2. V. G. Childe, *Introduction to Archaeology*, 1956, p. 72.

west Iberian province, although, as we shall see, they are the most common form in the north-eastern province. Covering mounds to these Iberian tombs, where they occur, are almost invariably round; the long barrow, which is so marked a feature of the British megalithic tombs, occurs frequently in France, and, as we have seen, in northern Europe, but is non-existent in Iberia.

The inhumed burials in the corbelled passage graves of Almeria are supplied with a rich variety of grave-goods. From the chamber tombs and associated settlements in Almeria come tools of copper (narrow flat axes and adzes, daggers, awls, saws) and stone (axe-heads, arrow-heads, and dagger and halberd blades superbly worked by pressure flaking, knives, sickle teeth) plaques of clay perforated at the four corners used as wrist guards or loom weights, pottery and ritual objects including owl-eyed figurines made of painted ox-phalanges, or on stone and ivory cylinders, and flat stone figures without faces. The pottery includes a great deal of undecorated ware as well as some decorated, and the decoration (sometimes painted but usually incised) includes knobs, the owl-eye and *oculi* motif found on the ritual objects, and conventionalized stags and human figures (generally done in 'hour-glass' form). Four out of the seventy-five tombs at Los Millares had beakers in them, and so did four others in Almeria.

The mention of beakers and of copper and stone implements in the last paragraph demands a short excursus on two general matters of prehistoric archaeology. It has been customary in archaeological description for over a hundred years to refer to remains of the prehistoric past in terms which imply the material mainly used for making tools and weapons, or rather the material that has survived in the archaeological record. The classification of man's archaeological remains into an Old Stone Age, a New Stone Age or Neolithic, a Bronze Age, and an Early Iron Age represents fairly generally the succession of material culture in Europe. For example, in Greece and in Crete the first peasant farmers are formally in the New Stone Age or

Neolithic, and are succeeded by an urban economy which was formally Bronze Age. A similar succession is true in Scandinavia and in southern England. We have already been discussing the Neolithic in northern Europe and seen that in Denmark it was a very long period which went on for a thousand years during eight hundred years of which megalithic tombs were in use. The beginnings of the Bronze Age (i.e. of bronze-using economies) in northern Europe may be dated between 1450 and 1400 B.C. The Bronze Age in Greece, however, began at 2400 or 2500 B.C. – the time when the Neolithic was beginning in Denmark; and the first Bronze Age culture of central Europe, that we have already referred to and named after Aunjetitz, began somewhere between 1700 and 1600 B.C. These terms, then, Stone Age, Bronze Age, and Early Iron Age, represent a simple linear succession of material culture; there is no absolute chronological implication in them.

The system as worked out in the nineteenth century needs considerable modification now, and this particularly applies to the study of megalithic tombs. First, some of the archaeological cultures can hardly be described as either Neolithic or Bronze Age; they belong to a time when metal tools were gradually coming into use but when no proper Bronze Age could yet be said to have started. To this culturally intermediate period between Neolithic and Bronze Age the term *Chalcolithic* is employed, and it is a very useful description of the megalithic cultures, or some of them. The term Chalcolithic is the proper description of the culture we have been describing at Los Millares and its neighbouring chamber tombs in Almeria.

Secondly, the earlier archaeologists who used and elaborated the classification of successive technological ages or stages were much influenced by preconceived ideas of evolution and progress. To them it was naturally explicit that a Bronze Age must succeed a Stone Age; they did not think in terms of degeneration or cultural regression – at least not many of them did. Nowadays while we see that the succession Neolithic, Chalcolithic, Bronze Age is well attested in many areas like the Near East and the Aegean, we are prepared to admit degeneration and regression. The evolutionary process can be reversed; useful arts can be lost, and we now think of the development or record of culture in historical terms and not by archaeological pre-conceptions. A group of people may have spread across Europe and started off with a knowledge of metal-working; they may have moved to an area where they could find no metal, or their few technicians in metal-working may have died out, leaving no tutored apprentices behind them. This group of people which was once formally Bronze Age has now become formally Neolithic. We now see that formally Neolithic cultures in Barbarian Europe may well be impoverished Chalcolithic cultures. We have already seen how the northern Neolithic cultures contained imitations in stone of bronze objects in other cultures – another form of technical impoverishment. So the whole story of the development of material culture in western Europe becomes much more complicated, but also, surely, more human and credible.

The second point of explanation concerns beakers. We cannot in a short book devoted to megalithic tombs explain all the archaeological categories and cultures to which we must make reference; and for explanation of things like 'funnel-necked beakers', to which we have already referred, or Chassey, Matera, and western Neolithic pottery to which reference will shortly be made, the reader must turn to the general books listed in the bibliography. But a word is necessary about beakers. The beaker is a drinking cup about 6 to 8 inches in height, of good quality red-brown decorated and burnished ware. Beakers are found widely distributed over western and central Europe; we have already referred to their appearance in Middle Neolithic C in northern Europe. They occur frequently in Iberia; and many people think that if they did not originate in Iberia, the Iberian peninsula was the centre of dispersal of beakers over the rest of Europe. Leisner and Savory divide the Iberian beakers into two groups, first the 'international' or 'classic' bell beaker – tall vessels with S-profiles and a simple pattern of pointillé lines forming horizontal bands diagonally hatched in alternate directions, and second, more squat beakers with the junction between neck and body more sharply demarcated, and decorated more elaborately by heavy pointillé work or continuous furrowing, commonly encrusted with a white substance. The first group is that which Leisner calls the 'Sea-movements Group', because its distribution must have been effected mainly by seaborne traffic (*Seeverkehr*). It belongs to the south and south-west of Spain, and spreads up to Galicia and across northern Spain to the Pyrenees; it is found in Andalucia, Portugal, Galicia, the Basque country, and northern Catalonia. The second group, which Leisner calls the 'Inland-movements Group', and Savory the Palmella-Ciempozuelos Group, belongs to the Spanish Meseta (especially the two Castiles) and southern Catalonia. It is associated with hemispherical bowls or platters often with heavy flattened rims, and even with pedestalled bowls, and is hardly found outside Spain, although decadent or hybrid examples are found across the French frontier in the Aude and Var departments.

Various ideas have been set forth regarding the origins of these beaker wares in Spain. Bosch Gimpera sees the Inland-movements Group, of Palmella-Ciempozuelos encrusted wares, giving rise to the 'international' bell beaker of Group I: most archaeologists see the reverse. Leisner would date Group I to 2200–1800 B.C., and Group II, developing out of it, to 1800–1400 B.C. Various ideas have also been set forth about the nature of this pottery; people talk about its owners and makers as the Beaker Folk. Leisner sees the 'international' bell beaker as belonging to a highly mobile hunting pastoral folk, and the Group II wares to sedentary agriculturists. To most people the 'international' bell beaker betokens a mobile seafaring and perhaps trading group of people. Our real point here concerns the relation of beakers and megalithic tombs, because when we come to France we shall find them closely related. In southern Iberia there are very few beakers in the Almerian collective tombs, and this was the point at which we began this brief excursus. Leisner would date the early development of Los Millares as contemporary with the development in south Spain of the 'international' bell beaker and to him this meant that we could give a horizon of roughly 2000–1800 B.C. for the bell beaker in Iberia. However this may be, what is important to appreciate here is that in their origins in southern Iberia the builders of the corbelled and megalithic passage graves and the Beaker Folk were not one and the same people.

Leisner divides the culture of the settlement and cemetery at Los Millares into two phases; his Phase II, which he dates from 1800–1400 B.C., has more complicated forms of tombs than Phase I, and an impoverishment of grave-goods. These tombs also lie farther off in the cemetery from the town. Beaker wares appear here during the transition from I to II and last into Phase II. It is time now, after our excursus on terminology and beakers, to return to the grave-goods of the other Iberian tombs.

The tombs of the Guadix–Gor–Gorafe area on the plateau of Granada contain grave-goods like those of the Almerian coast – *oculi* vases, flat stone idols, phalange idols, ribbed cylinder-headed pins, as well as, very occasionally, some beakers. Some tombs in this area, like Los Eriales, contain pottery and bronzes characteristic not of the Chalcolithic Millaran culture but of a succeeding Bronze Age culture, the Argaric, so called in Spain after the site of El Argar, also in Almeria. The date of this Argaric culture is generally thought to be from 1500 B.C. onwards and it seems reasonable to suppose that in the Guadix–Gorafe–Gor area collective tombs were being built in the centuries following the middle of the second millennium B.C.

The collective tombs of the Algarve in south Portugal have yielded flat copper adzes, notched copper daggers with midribs, awls and saws of copper, very fine hollow-based arrow-heads of flint, and hammer beads – all like the Millaran grave-goods. The pottery is all undecorated, mainly round-bottomed, of the pottery family called Western Neolithic Ware. No beakers have been found in these south Portuguese tombs. Beads of amber, jet, and callais have been found; the last is a sort of turquoise whose origin is uncertain and which is thought to come from coastal outcrops in the south of Brittany now lying beneath the sea. The amber from northern Europe and the callais from Brittany would have been traded along the Atlantic trade routes pioneered or developed by the megalith builders.

The culture of the chamber tomb builders in the Tagus estuary as revealed by the rock-cut tombs of Palmella and Alapraia is much like that of the Millaran tombs, except that here metal tools and weapons are rare and consist mainly of curious tanged copper points or arrow-heads – the so-called Palmella point. The industry of the Tagus folk is more 'lithic' than Chalcolithic; it contains stone axes, adzes, and wonderfully worked flint arrow-heads and halberds or spear blades. There are bone cylinder-headed pins, clay plaques perforated at the four corners, and objects of gold, callais, amber, and ivory. The pottery from these rock-cut tombs includes plain round-bottomed and carinated pots comparable with those in Millaran and the Algarve tombs, i.e. Western Neolithic Ware; but there is also a great prominence of beaker ware, including the Palmella–Ciempozuelos encrusted variety. The ritual objects from these mid-Tagus tombs include phalange and cylinder idols, and schist sandals, as well as the very famous schist plaque idols and 'croziers'.

The grave-goods of the megalithic passage graves and single polygonal chambers of central and northern Portugal are much poorer than the rich cemeteries of the Lisbon and Algarve area; stone axes and plain and round-bottomed or carinated pots are most common, sherds of beaker pottery are found, occasionally the form of copper dagger known as the west European tanged dagger, cylinder-headed pins, beads of callais, and schist idols and croziers.

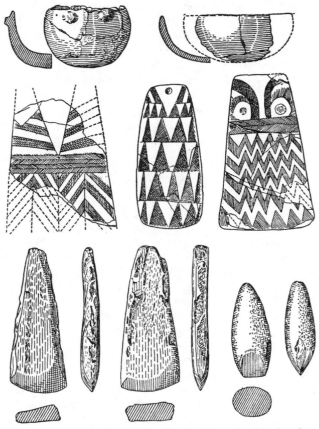

Fig. 10 – Grave-goods from the chambered tomb of Farisoa I
(*after G. and V. Leisner*)

There are also flat-bottomed and handled pots, which belong to chronological and cultural horizon comparable
with the Algaric Bronze Age of south-eastern Spain, so that
some at least of the interior and north Portuguese sites
were being made or used after 1500 B.C.

We have seen that the ritual objects found in the Iberian
chamber tombs preserve in a stylized way some sort of cult

figure, represented by idols of bone and flat plaques, and by the *oculi* motifs on pottery. Four of the southern Spanish chamber tombs have designs incised on the walls of the chambers themselves. The Cueva de Menga at Antequera has curious stylized figures of crosses and semicircles. The two dolmens at Soto in Huelva province have a variety of symbols on them including an unmistakable *oculi* face, while a tomb at Jerez de los Caballeros has rayed suns. In northern Portugal and in the Galicia–Asturias region of north-western Spain there are some twenty to twenty-five chamber tombs with art on their walls, and about fifteen of these – a particular group each side of the Douro – have designs in paint; these and one or two other painted sites in northern Spain (Gangas de Oñis is one) are the only examples of painted decoration known to me in Iberian megaliths. Some of these designs preserve the owl-face of the de Soto dolmens and the pottery; other designs consist of zigzag lines which compare with the geometrical decoration on the schist plaques. The megalithic tomb of Orca dos Juncais near Vizeu in north Portugal has painted on it very naturalistic animals belonging to a style of art very different from that represented by the cult objects of southern Iberia. It is quite obvious that the megalith builders of northern Portugal and north-western Spain were in cultural contact with other artistic traditions; and *per contra*, the characteristic megalithic mural art is found on sites other than chamber tombs. On a slab of rock from north Portugal are to be found the same zigzag lines associated with spirals, but the spiral itself does not occur on any tomb in Iberia. Single stones have been found fashioned into figures in the owl-face goddess tradition; these statue menhirs in Iberia occur mainly in north Portugal and at one rock shelter – that of Peña Tu – the owl-faced goddess figure is painted and engraved, and near by, though, of course, not necessarily contemporaneous, is the representation of a tanged west European metal dagger such as is occasionally found in the north-west Iberian megaliths.

The Megalith Builders of Western Europe

We have now given a brief account of the chamber tombs of the south and west Iberian megalithic province. What explanation in historical terms can be given for these tombs, their grave-goods, their different forms and constructions, and their mobiliary and mural art? Here we embark on the second great controversial issue in the study of European megalithic tombs. The French archaeologist Cartailhac first analysed the Iberian megaliths, and did so by fitting them in to Montelius's classification of the chamber tombs of northern Europe; he adopted Montelius's evolutionary sequence as well, and argued that the single megalithic chambers of Iberia came first and then developed into passage graves. This thesis was developed and elaborated by Leeds, Wilke, Obermaier, Aberg, and most of all by the Catalan archaeologist Bosch Gimpera. These archaeologists were, of course, much affected by the notion of evolutionary progress in the elaboration of tomb-types and in material culture; they therefore thought the 'Neolithic' grave-goods of the north Portuguese single chambers must necessarily be earlier than the Chalcolithic grave-goods of the south Spanish and Portuguese tombs, and that 'simple' structures like the orthostat-walled and trabeate-roofed tombs of north Portugal and Galicia must of necessity be earlier than the 'complex' and 'elaborate' structures of southern Iberia, particularly the magnificent corbel vaulted passage graves. I have put some of these words in inverted commas because whenever writers speak of primitive and complex, simple and elaborate, in relation to megalithic tombs we are getting near the point when we should ask sharply whether these terms are being used subjectively to denote observer-imposed prejudices.

Bosch Gimpera regarded the whole Iberian development as indigenous; he boldly derived all the Iberian chamber tombs from the single chambers of Galicia and north Portugal, and envisaged a dual spread from this north-western corner of Iberia, the one east along the north coast of Spain to the Basque–Catalan area, the second south and south-east to Alcalá and Los Millares. As this tomb idea spreads south it becomes more complicated; the single chamber without passage gives rise to the megalithic passage grave, and this to the corbelled passage grave and the rock-cut tomb. Alcalá and Los Millares then stand at the height of a magnificent local Iberian development – the full flowering of which is late in the Chalcolithic period and the beginnings of which are well back in the Neolithic. To put his thesis in terms of absolute chronology, Bosch Gimpera suggested that the north Portuguese and Galician single chambers date between 3000 and 2500 B.C., Palmella between 2500 and 2300, and Alcalá and Los Millares after this date.

For a while this explanation of the origin and development of Iberian chamber-tomb architecture was widely held, if often with certain modifications. The most important of these concerned the corbelled-roofed surface tombs, or cupola tombs (or *tholoi*) as some people have called them. The resemblance between the Millaran and Alcalán tombs on the one hand and on the other the Mycenaean *tholoi* of Greece, had often been noticed : Siret pointed it out and proposed to derive the Millaran tombs from the Mycenaean. Joseph Déchelette argued against this; but the comparison in form and function, if not in details of construction and use, remained valid, and, as knowledge grew of the collective tombs of the Aegean, more and more archaeologists were impressed by the similarities between the Spanish tombs and the *tholoi*. So much so that archaeologists like Wilke and Obermaier, while accepting the general correctness of the classic thesis expounded by Leeds and Bosch Gimpera, yet held that the corbelled passage graves had been introduced from the east Mediterranean. These archaeologists still argued for a north Portuguese–Galician 'Neolithic' origin for Iberian megalithic architecture, but an east Mediterranean origin for the corbelled passage graves.

Let us for the sake of convenience call these two points of view the classic Leeds–Bosch Gimpera view and the Wilke–Obermaier view. Then, in the early thirties of the present century a new point of view was advanced, and first by a group of English archaeologists, notably Forde, Fleure, and Peake; it was a point of view rapidly adopted by Gordon Childe. From this new viewpoint it appeared that the single polygonal chambers of north Portugal and Galicia could equally well represent degenerate and impoverished, and not primitive and undeveloped cultures. These writers suggested that the earliest chamber tombs in Iberia were in fact the fine south Iberian corbelled passage graves and rock-cut tombs, and that these were translated into megalithic tombs in areas where suitable stone for dry walling did not exist or when the complicated technique of corbel vaulting was no longer practised, or where it was not easy to cut tombs in the rock. The megalithic passage grave was an Iberian invention which flourished in the hinterland and the polygonal and rectangular single chambers of north Portugal–Galicia and of the Cordoba–Granada inland areas were in fact the latest form of chamber tomb. This is a complete reversal of the classic Leeds–Bosch Gimpera point of view, and it makes the 'primitive' Neolithic cultures of the early third millennium B.C. into impoverished Chalcolithic cultures of the middle or late second millennium B.C. It is when there can be such variation in the interpretation of megalithic tombs and archaeological material, that the general reader sometimes begins to wonder whether there is any safe foothold in the shifting quicksands of controversy, and thinks of the dons in Siegfried Sassoon's poem who 'argue easily round megaliths'.

But the possibilities of interpretation and disagreement were not exhausted by the production of the Forde–Fleure view. We have already mentioned the views of the Leisners; after a long and detailed study of the chamber tombs of southern Spain and Portugal they have produced a point of view which differs from the others. They draw attention to the existence in south-eastern Spain of tombs which are closed chambers in round mounds and which date from as early as the Millaran passage graves. These, they think, might give a context which provides a local origin for the Millaran passage graves. The Leisners also argue that in the Huelva and south Portuguese region the megalithic tombs are earlier in date than the corbelled tombs; they have made a special study of the Reguengos region in east Portugal on the right bank of the Guadiana river, where they describe 134 passage graves – all, except two, megalithic. These two exceptions are Anta 2 of Commenda 36 and Anta 1 of Farisoa III, and here the Leisners found two dry-walled corbel-vaulted tombs inserted in round mounds which already contained orthostatic passage graves and were therefore later than them. From these two tombs and an analysis of grave-goods the Leisners argue for a native megalithic tradition though not, as in the Leeds–Bosch Gimpera thesis, primarily displayed in north-western Spain : they see this tradition on the inland Meseta plateau which was settled by pastoralists using microliths, cylindrical axes, and adzes and building small megalithic cists and galleries. Actually this stage has been distinguished for some while in Portugal by Do Paço, Correia, and Heleno in the Alemtejo area where it is represented by small oblong or oval chambers with very small passages set in round mounds which contain microliths, cylindrical axes, and adzes, but no engraved schist plaques and other distinctive passage grave objects. While the Portuguese archaeologists we have cited have not insisted that this Alemtejo culture is necessarily earlier than the megalithic passage graves, the Leisners do.

The Leisner theory then is a dual origin for the Iberian collective tombs, first in south-east Spain from the closed round chambers of the Almerian area, and second from the native megalithic cists of central and north-western Spain. The corbelled passage grave develops out of the south-east Spanish closed round chambers, and the megalithic passage grave out of the western megalithic cists. The essentials of this view, which assumes a native west European megalithic tradition, and a Spanish origin for the corbelled tombs, has interesting possibilities. May it not be that while

The Megalith Builders of Western Europe

Siret's comparison was right, his direction was wrong, and that the east Mediterranean *tholoi* were derived from the Iberian tombs? In an interesting review of the work of the Leisners, Professor Piggott says he is encouraged 'to support the thesis of a derivation of the Mycenaean chamber-tomb tradition from the west'.[1] There have always been people anxious to react from the doctrine of *ex oriente lux*, and recently Dr Dominic Joseph Wolfel of Vienna has argued for a great western European and north-west African tradition of religion, culture, and life in prehistoric times: to him, collective tombs and the magico-religious art of the collective tombs originated in the west and probably in Spain and spread from Iberia to the east Mediterranean.'[2]

What position can the general reader be advised to take in the interpretation of the Spanish and Portuguese collective tombs? He has the classic Leeds–Bosch Gimpera view, the Wilke–Obermaier view, the Forde–Fleure view, and the Leisner view, and in assessing these views he must remember that we have accepted the independent origin of megalithic tombs in Early Neolithic C of northern Europe. The two things to keep foremost in the mind are that while the use of large stones may occur independently in different places, collective burial in a chamber tomb is surely a complicated and religious idea, and that this religious idea is manifested not only in burial and funerary custom and architecture but in the delineation of a cult figure. To my way of thinking the disputes about typology and tomb types become academic exercises if we forget that the great megalithic tomb builders of western Europe were imbued by a religious faith and were devotees of a goddess whose face glares out from pot and phalange idol and the dark shadows of the tomb walls, whose image is twisted into the geometry of Portuguese schist plaques and the rich carv-

1. *Antiquity*, 1953, p. 142.
2. Wölfel's views are set out in a section of Franz König's *Christus und die Religioner der Erde*. They are summarized and discussed by Sir John Myres in *Antiquity*, 1953, p. 3.

ings of Gavrinnis and New Grange. The question turns on megalithic art. The distribution of Iberian megalithic art, mobiliary and parietal, is a coastal one. The cult-figure is seen at its best and freshest in the dry-walled tombs of southern Iberia and appears less recognizable as we move west and north into Portugal and Galicia. What is more, this figure has very strong parallels in the east Mediterranean and the Near East, in contexts earlier than our earliest Spanish ones. I find it very difficult to believe that our Spanish goddess and our *oculi* motifs do not come from the early goddess figures of Cyprus, Crete, the Cyclades, and western Anatolia. While recognizing, then, the existence of pre-collective tomb cultures in western Europe, as in Denmark, that could have had megalithic cists, it still seems to me that the Forde–Fleure theory is the most plausible. Settlers arrived in southern Iberia from the east Mediterranean somewhere before 2000 B.C., bringing with them the custom of collective tomb burial and a strong religious belief in an Earth Mother Goddess. Their first settlements we can find in the Almerian region; Los Millares is of a type of small east Mediterranean township transported to Spain. From these centres in east and south Spain and perhaps also the Tagus estuary the Iberian Chalcolithic culture developed and, as it developed, perhaps in contact with earlier aborigines who built megalithic cists, the megalithic passage grave was evolved, and, out of these developments, the tombs of northern Portugal and Galicia and the Cordoba–Granada area, some of which certainly date after 1500 B.C.

The first tombs were then rock-cut tombs and dry-walled tombs (including the closed dry-walled tombs which the Leisners think indigenous in south-east Spain). This does not mean that all rock-cut tombs are necessarily early – the Alcaide group near Antequera contains Argaric material – or that all dry-walled corbelled passage graves are necessarily earlier than all megalithic passage graves – the Leisners' evidence from Reguengos is conclusive on this point, although the two sites they mention are rather poor examples of the corbel-vault tradition. This is how the facts seem to me at present to be best interpreted. But no one should pretend, in the face of even this brief recital of the contending theories about Iberian megaliths, that the Forde–Fleure theory, even modified as I have suggested, is more than a useful working hypothesis.

It remains to say a few words only about the remaining province of Iberian megalithic architecture. In the north-east of Spain there are megalithic tombs in the Basque provinces, in Aragon, and in Catalonia. These have been specially studied by Professor Pericot y García. There are no corbel vaults in these regions and no rich grave-goods with owl faces. The tombs are mainly rectangular or polygonal single chambers with a few megalithic passage graves, some V-shaped passage graves and entrance graves, and a few longer rectangular tombs some with segmentations which should perhaps be described as gallery graves. Pericot argues that the Pyrenean and Catalan megalithic culture lasted from 2500 B.C. to 1000 B.C. and the button handles and Polada affinities of the material from the rect-angular chambers shows clearly the relative position of these monuments in the sequence of Iberian collective tombs. There seem to be three influences at work in this north-eastern Spanish province. The first is across the north of Spain from Galicia and Asturias; the second is up the south-east coast from Almeria by sea to Catalonia; and the third comes in from southern France, and can only be understood when we have studied the collective tombs of southern France and the western Mediterranean islands to which we now turn.

1. (a) A *hunebed* in Holland and (b) a Portuguese *anta*.
Two typical free-standing megalithic tombs

2. Two Irish free-standing megalithic tombs: (a) in Brenanstown, County Dublin, and (b) in Proleek, County Louth

3. Interior views of two gallery graves: (a) at Baigneux, Saumur, Maine-et-Loire, and (b) at Stoney Littleton, Somerset

4. The corbelled roof of the main chamber at New Grange, Ireland

5. Portholes in tombs in Gloucestershire: (a) at Avening and (b) at Rodmarton

6. (a) The passage grave of Torche-en-Plomeur, Finistère, and (b) the entrance to the rock-cut tomb of the Grotte de la Source, near Arles

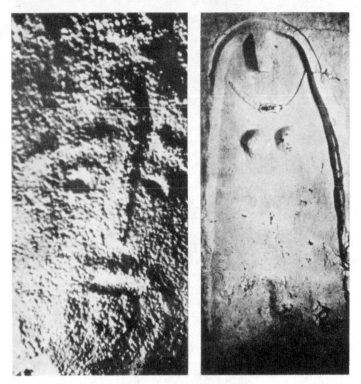

7. Figures of the funerary goddess:
(a) on the underside of the capstone of the Déhus tomb, Guernsey, and
(b) at the entrance to one of the Courjeonnet tombs, Marne

8. Examples of megalithic art: (a) from New Grange, Ireland, and (b) from Gavr'innis, Brittany

4

THE WEST MEDITERRANEAN

WE have already, in discussing the megalithic tombs of
eastern Spain, been dealing with one side of the west Mediterranean, and in our next chapter we shall deal with the
south French tombs along the northern edge of the west
Mediterranean sea. The west coast of Italy, which forms
the eastern wall of the west Mediterranean, was not settled
by the builders of collective tombs except for a cemetery
of such tombs discovered accidentally by American and
British troops at Gaudo, near Paestum, and excavated more
thoroughly later by Sestieri. This cemetery consisted of
twenty tombs all cut out of the soft limestone; they were
dome-shaped chambers approached by a pit entrance and
contained from two to twenty-five burials deposited either
squatting around the walls or crouching in the central area.
The grave-goods comprised pottery, flint implements, and
two riveted and round-heeled copper daggers. The pottery
includes *askoi*, the so-called salt-cellars, and beaker-shaped
pots with concave mouths very like pots from Siculan I
and Troy II contexts. Sestieri would on this evidence date
the Gaudo tombs to the period designated in Cretan prehistory as from Early Minoan III to Middle Minoan I,
which is, according to our present chronologies, at the
turn of the third and second millennia. It does look as if in
Paestum we have evidence of a settlement of Aegean
people somewhere between 2400 and 1900 B.C. Apart from
tombs near Bari, to which reference will be made later,
Italy has no further interest for us. Along the north coast
of Africa, particularly in Algeria, there are to be found at
the present day large numbers of megalithic structures,
mainly rectangular in plan, which if found isolated in

The Megalith Builders of Western Europe

Galicia or west Wales or south Jutland would be described as single rectangular chambers or 'dolmens'. But the Algerian megaliths seem to belong to the centuries immediately before and after the beginning of the Christian era, and do not concern us here immediately except as an example of megalithic tomb architecture which seems to have developed independently here in Africa Minor, probably at least a thousand years after the megalithic tombs we have been describing in Spain and Portugal.

It is the islands of the west Mediterranean that were the main centres of the collective tomb builders in prehistoric times – the Balearics, Sardinia, Sicily, and Malta in particular. Corsica has very few megalithic tombs. Pantelleria, a large volcanic island in the Sicilian Channel between Tunis and Sicily, has curious megalithic tombs known locally as *sesi*, which look like passage graves in plan, and have circular chambers with corbelled roofs. The finest of these, the Sese Grande, is an oval mound with a maximum diameter of over 60 feet covering and containing twelve passage graves and reminds one forcibly of the Fontenay-le-Marmion site in Normandy. Let us turn now to Sicily.

Paolo Orsi distinguished in Sicilian prehistory four Siculan periods, and a pre-Siculan or Neolithic period before Siculan I. This early Neolithic culture is known as the Stentinello culture and is characterized by little fortified villages, like Stentinello itself; the pottery includes undecorated, round-bottomed and carinated ware much like the western Neolithic pottery of Iberia and western France as well as pottery decorated by impression or incision before firing – the decoration includes the impressions of cardium shells, zigzag lines, and stylizations of the human figure or of eyes. The graves of the Stentinello culture are pit graves or natural caves and the communal pit-cave tomb seems a part of this early Neolithic context in the mid-Mediterranean which is in terms of absolute chronology somewhere in the second half of the third millennium B.C. The Siculan I phase which succeeds the Stentinello Neolithic has recently been studied in detail by Bernabò

Brea, who distinguishes three intrusive cultures: all, he argues, of Aegean origin, and named Serraferlicchio, San Ippolito, and Castelluccio. He argues that these have a common origin in the Aegean, but that the Aegean traits they demonstrate are so divergent as to prove that these cultures affected Sicily at different times; all represent a 'genuine movement of colonization, preceding at a distance of more than a millennium the very similar phenomenon of the Greek colonization'.[1]

Castelluccio is the latest of these three cultures to be established, and it flourished in the south-east corner of Sicily, mainly around Syracuse. All the tombs of the Castelluccio people were collective; small round chambers cut in the rock with a rounded vault. The diameters of these chambers are from 5 to 12 feet; they are approached through an antechamber and a round or rectangular opening closed by a wall of dry-stone walling or by a megalithic slab. A few of these megalithic closing slabs have well-executed designs of spirals and lozenges (Fig. 11). The tombs contain the remains of several dozens of individuals. Brea dates the Castelluccio culture to between 1800 and 1600 B.C. and emphasizes the close similarities between its pottery and some of the Cycladic and Middle Helladic Greek pottery. Ten examples are known from the Castelluccio contexts of curious objects about 6 inches long called 'bossed bone plaques'; similar objects have been found in Troy in contexts that seem probably to be Troy II and one at Lerna in Greece in a context on the borderline between Early Helladic and Middle Helladic, i.e. about 1800 B.C. The Castelluccio plaques thus help to date the culture, although they themselves are decorated with zigzag lines and *oculi* motifs and seem to be in the same general tradition as the cult objects of Almeria we have already discussed.

In Sicily, then, we have clear evidence of Aegean settlers who built collective tombs in and around 2000 B.C. They

1. Bernabò Brea in *Annual Report, University of London Institute of Archaeology*, 1950, p. 23.

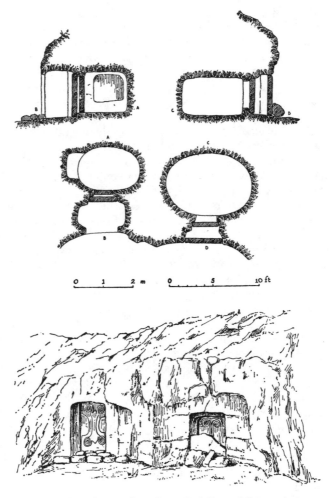

Fig. 11 – (*Top*) Plans and sections of tombs and (*bottom*) stone entrances to rock-cut tombs at Castelluccio, Sicily (*after Brea*)

84

were not the first post-Mesolithic peoples in the island, nor the only ones. Other Chalcolithic communities existed in Sicily also of east Mediterranean origin, who did not build collective tombs. Nor are all the collective tombs of Sicily part of the Castelluccio culture. In the succeeding phase of Sicilian prehistory, Siculan II, chamber tombs continue using masonry blocks and stone pillars with plans which make them strictly speaking *tholoi* : such are the tombs at Thapsos and Pantalica. Aegean imports date these tombs to Late Minoan III, i.e. somewhere between 1400 and 1200 B.C.

The megalithic monuments of Malta (and its neighbouring island of Gozo) have for long excited the interest of archaeologist and traveller, and attention has been concentrated on the great so-called 'temples' like Hal Tarxien, Mnaidra, and Hagiar Kim in Malta, and the Gigantija on Gozo. These monuments are very large and impressive; they are, indeed, truly megalithic in the most literal sense of the word; they consist in plan of a central passage or gallery from which pairs of transepts open out and end in an apsidal or terminal chamber. Several of the stones of these great megalithic 'temples' are finely decorated with spirals, but also with realistic animal designs which are not found elsewhere in the art of the west Mediterranean and west European collective tomb builders. The objects found in the excavation of these great sites have included figures of obese ladies, perhaps goddess or priestess figures, and some have suggested – the idea is not quite fantastic – that the plans of these monuments represent the outline of a fat goddess. The hypogeum of Hal Saflieni on Malta has also excited a great deal of attention; it is a most complicated rock-cut tomb with painted spirals on its roof which is estimated to have held the remains of several thousand bodies.

The Hal Tarxien megalithic monuments were excavated by Sir Themistocles Zammit soon after they were discovered by accident in 1914. He found that the original material remains were covered by three feet of silt, which had spread over the site during the time when the monuments were heaps of ruins, and that then the site had been used as an open cremation-cemetery by people who used metal. The triangular copper daggers with two or four rivet-holes, flat and slightly flanged axes with expanding blades, and circular section awls found in this cremation-cemetery of Hal Tarxien Period II are the oldest metal objects found in Malta. The original megalithic monuments

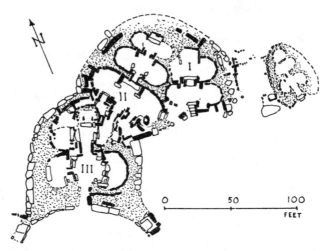

Fig. 12 – Plan of megalithic temples at Hal Tarxien, Malta

here (Hal Tarxien I), and the other megalithic monuments in Malta we have mentioned, contain no metal and are formally Neolithic. In textbook statements of the prehistory of Malta until recently it has been customary to refer to a long Neolithic period in Malta characterized by the great temples and the Hal Saflieni hypogeum, succeeded by the Bronze Age beginning with the Hal Tarxien cremation-cemetery; this beginning is variously dated at 2000 B.C. or later and the extent of the 'Neolithic' or 'Megalithic' Phase has never been made precise. In the 1948 edition of his

The West Mediterranean

Dawn of European Civilization, Professor Gordon Childe wrote:

> The 'Bronze Age' invasion of Malta can accordingly be placed anywhere between 1800 and 800 B.C. No convincing grounds can be advanced for preferring one or other limit. It is more honest to admit that the age of the several Maltese cultures, and consequently Malta's role in prehistoric Europe, cannot be correctly estimated on the available evidence.

Since these words were written J. D. Evans has been working in Malta, and from studying the pottery sequence there and relating the whole of Maltese prehistory to the detailed knowledge now available of Sicilian prehistory he has been able to work out a scheme which is most plausible, and which helps us to understand the role of Malta in prehistoric Europe; it throws a great light on the evolution of megalithic architecture in Europe as a whole. He emphasizes that the great stone 'temples' represent the *floruit* of the Maltese megalithic culture and that to understand them we must go back to their origins. He sees the first colonization of Malta by a people of Stentinello affiliation probably during the last centuries of the third millennium B.C. These first settlers had rock-cut tombs and soon translated them (perhaps because of the availability of easily cut limestone) into above-ground megalithic structures. These develop into the great stone structures of Gigantija and Hal Tarxien, but it was not an isolated development; the Maltese megalith builders had contacts with the outside world, and the running spirals of Hal Tarxien must surely, as Evans and others have argued, be inspired by the spirals on the shaft graves at Mycenae. He would then date the *floruit* of the Maltese megalithic culture at about the sixteenth century B.C. and make it synchronous in part with the Castelluccio culture of Sicily. Hal Tarxien itself yielded in a context which is either right at the end of the megalithic occupation or at the beginning of the 'Bronze Age' cemetery one of the bossed bone plaques which were common in Castelluccio contexts.

If Evans's analysis of the Maltese megalithic culture is right we are presented then here with a sequence of tomb construction and culture supported by outside contacts and well dated in relative and absolute terms, which may well bid fair to be as important in the general theory of megalithic tombs as the disputed sequences in northern Europe and Iberia which we have been discussing. We have in Malta small circular rock-cut tombs developing into surface megalithic tombs, becoming elaborated as monuments of the Hal Tarxien–Gigantija type. Evans has also shown by excavation that the 'dolmens' of Malta, simple megalithic single chambers, are late in his established sequence of pottery. This classic Maltese sequence has only been in existence a few years, and it is always possible that, as in Iberia, schools of thought will arise which will try to reverse it. It seems unlikely to me, because owing to the mid-Mediterranean position of Malta and the researches which have gone on in the last ten years in Sicily, the Liparis, and south Italy, the Maltese sequence is securely anchored to the absolute chronology of the east Mediterranean, and is not a typological iceberg floating in the uncertain seas of Iberian and northern European chronology, liable to turn upside down in the melting heat of fresh analysis.

One final point about these Maltese megaliths. The great structures like Hal Tarxien and Mnaidra are always referred to as 'temples', and there is no evidence of their sepulchral use. Yet they developed out of rock-cut and megalithic tombs. We must bear this in mind when we look at some of the west European megalithic tombs like the great gallery graves of the Loire Valley and eastern Brittany. They, too, may have been non-sepulchral in purpose. And the very evolution of tomb into temple in Malta reminds us forcibly that all along these early tombs had a ritual and religious purpose. Whether the Maltese temples were ever roofed, and, if so, how, is a much-disputed question. No surviving temple is roofed, although the beginnings of corbel courses of large stones are found and the model of what may be a megalithic temple was found at Mgarr; it certainly is roofed with what look like megalithic slabs.[1] If so, these must have been extremely large and it is surprising that they have all disappeared. Let us turn from these minor mysteries to the major problems of the Sardinian collective tombs.

The collective tombs of Sardinia are of two types – rock-cut and surface tombs. The rock-cut tombs range from hemispherical rock-cut chambers entered through a narrow portal from a pit or slope (identical in form with the Sicilian and Cycladic collective tombs) through more complicated plans, culminating in the remarkable tombs of the cemetery of Anghelu Ruju near Alghero in the north of the island. These rock-cut tombs go by various folk-names but are generally referred to as *domus di gianas* – the houses of the fairies or witches. The surface tombs on the other hand are generally referred to as *tombe di giganti*, giants' graves. There are also structures that are intermediate between these, being half rock-cut and half surface.

The *tombe di giganti* are cyclopean-built long mounds of stone (with megaliths frequently used orthostatically) containing a long burial chamber usually corbel-roofed but sometimes trabeate-roofed which, in the terminology of western European megalithic monuments, can only be described as a gallery grave. Sometimes the gallery grave opens on to a straight wall as at Su Coveccu and S'enna sa Vacca (see Fig. 13), sometimes on to a slightly curved or crescentic or V-shaped façade (as in Goronna South and Corongianus), sometimes on to a semicircular forecourt defined by curved walls or horns sweeping out from the sidewalls of the mound of stones (as in Sella Fontana Binu and Muraguada). It is these 'horned cairns' that have particularly attracted the interest of western European archaeologists interested in monuments with horned forecourts in

1. For a readily accessible good photograph of this Mgarr model see *Antiquity*, 1942, facing p. 24.

the British Isles. Often the central stone in the middle of the forecourt of these Sardinian giants' graves is very large, has recessed panels, and a 'kennel-hole' opening at the bottom communicating with the gallery grave beyond. In

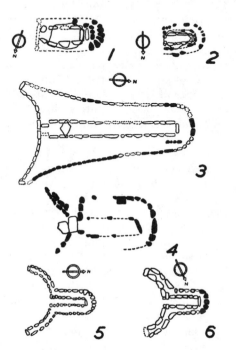

Fig. 13 – Giants' graves from Sardinia

(1) Su Coveccu   (4) Corongianus, Coloru
(2) S'enna sa Vacca   (5) Sella Fontana Binu
(3) Goronna South   (6) Muraguada

addition to these giants' graves there are also in Sardinia single rectangular chambers usually referred to in the literature on Sardinia as 'dolmens'.

In common with most other areas which have many and varied collective tombs, Sardinia has been a field for typological exercises, and its tombs have been arranged in a variety of sequences. Montelius, Taramelli, and Mackenzie assumed that the Sardinian 'dolmens' came first and gradually developed into the larger and more complicated gallery graves; Oliver Davies, on the other hand, insisted that there was no evidence for assuming that the small single Sardinian burial chambers were necessarily earlier than the giants' graves. It is only in the last few years and as a result of fresh studies by Massimo Pallottino, that the chronological position of the giants' graves has become fairly certain. There now seems little doubt that the majority of the giants' graves in Sardinia date between 1500 and 800 B.C., and are contemporary in part with the remarkable *nuraghi* of which there are so many thousands in Sardinia. *Nuraghi* are cyclopean circular towers either standing alone or as part of a farm or village of small dry-walled houses. The Nuraghic Civilization, pre-Greek and pre-Phoenician, is one of the most interesting features of Sardinian prehistory; the cyclopean towers themselves are remarkable and so are the Sardinian or Sardo-Etruscan bronze figures belonging to it. It now seems likely that the giants' graves belong at least to the first half of the Nuraghic Civilization.

The rock-cut tombs are earlier, and with them we must include natural caves used as burial places, such as S. Michele di Ozieri and San Bartolomeo, which was a cave used as a habitation and which had beneath a layer including beakers and west European tanged daggers and a flat axe of copper, a funerary level with round-bottomed and carinated undecorated pottery as well as pottery decorated in a late Neolithic style found in Malta. The cemetery of Anghelu Ruju, with its thirty-one collectively used tombs, contains material which may be compared with both levels at San Bartolomeo as well as material which occurs in the Nuraghic Civilization. There seems to be a general synchronism between some of the late Chalcolithic material at Anghelu Ruju, part of Castelluccio and the *floruit* of Maltese megalithic architecture. The beginnings of the Sardinian rock-cut tombs may well go back to 2000 B.C. or before. The plan of one or two tombs in

Sardinia can be closely paralleled in Malta (e.g. Corradino) and we have already seen there are contacts with prehistoric Maltese pottery. On the other hand the marble statuettes from the Sardinian rock-cut tombs are more closely paralleled in the Aegean and the ox-horn motifs carved on the walls of the Anghelu Ruju also point to the Aegean. Some Italian archaeologists have argued that Sardinia was settled by Minoans about 2000 B.C. : and it is difficult not to see in the rock-cut tombs and in Anghelu Ruju particularly a direct east Mediterranean influence. It is probably these east Mediterranean colonists, perhaps in touch with Malta, who developed the cyclopean giants' graves at a later period.

In many ways the collective tombs of the Balearics are comparable with those of Sardinia; they consist of rock-cut tombs and of cyclopean tombs or *navetas*, but in detail the comparison is not exact. The rock-cut tombs occur mainly on Mallorca; they are long tombs often with subsidiary chambers, antechambers, and rectangular forecourts. The tombs are sometimes broken up by cross stalls or *septae* and often have lateral rock-cut benches. Hemp observed that one of the rock-cut tombs at Son Caulellas had a sort of barrow on the surface of the ground above it. The *navetas* occur both in Mallorca and Menorca, but the better known and better preserved examples are to be found in the smaller and less highly cultivated island. Good examples in Menorca are the *navetas* of Rafal Rubi, and that of Es Tudons, which is 45 feet long by 15 feet high. Inside, the *navetas* are replicas of the rock-cut tombs, with corridor, antechamber, and chamber (Fig. 14).

The grave-goods from the rock-cut tombs and from the *navetas* belong to a culture of Argaric affinities; many of these have been poorly excavated, but there is no material at present known to me to suggest that there was a Chalcolithic period for these collective tombs. No beakers or associated material have been found in the Balearics except for some doubtful sherds from the rock-cut tomb of Felanitz and a V-perforated button from the rock-cut tomb of Son Mulet. Apart from pottery which looks like Argaric or sub-Argaric material there are coarse, flat-bottomed flower-pots like the secondary Neolithic ware of France. We must, I think, here agree that the Balearic rock-cut and surface collective tombs must in the main be later than 1500 B.C.

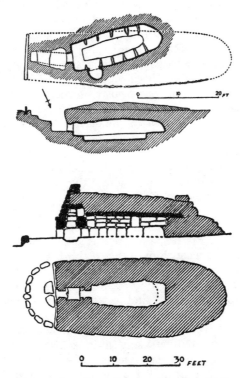

Fig. 14 – Plans and sections of rock-cut tomb in Mallorca (*top*) and *naveta* in Menorca (*bottom*) (*after Hemp*)

There is no very clear evidence of direct east-Mediterranean contact except for a Middle Cycladic beaked jug found at Iviza.

Maluquer de Motes has divided the prehistory of the Balearics into two phases. The first, which he calls the Argaric, comprises the rock-cut tombs and *navetas* we have been discussing; the second, which he calls the Talayotic and which probably began between 1200 and 1000 B.C., was flourishing in the eighth century B.C., and carried on through the Early Iron Age into the Roman period. This phase is characterized not only by cyclopean-built settlements of a village kind, but the talayots themselves – small fortified settlements with massive walls, square on Mallorca, round on Menorca, and taulas, curious horizontal stones lying across the head of an upright stone like a giant T or Tau cross which have been variously interpreted as parts of sanctuaries or the centre-posts of buildings. What concerns us here is that in the use of large stones the cyclopean and megalithic traditions of the earlier Argaric phase continued in the Balearics.

It may well be that future work in the Balearics will reveal a pre-Argaric phase for the rock-cut tombs or some of them; until then we must draw the conclusion that the Balearics were rather late in the developing traditions of collective tombs in the west Mediterranean. Whence came the settlers who perhaps as late as 1600 or 1500 B.C. occupied the Balearics? Spain itself is a possibility, Sardinia another, and the south of France a third. The matter is not one for which there is an easy answer. It has been suggested that the small group of megalithic monuments that exists in south-east Italy and to which a brief reference has already been made were derived from the gallery graves of southern France; we shall see in the next chapter that collective-tomb builders settled in southern France and that southern France has evidence of direct contacts with the east Mediterranean. It may well be that after this south French Chalcolithic culture had been established settlers from southern France moving back along well-known west-Mediterranean routes, settled in the Balearics on one hand and in south-east Italy on the other.

5

FRANCE

5,000 → 5,500 tombs

WHEN Joseph Déchelette wrote his *Manuel d'archéologie préhistorique celtique et gallo-romaine*, the first volume of which was published in 1908, but which still remains the chief work of reference on French prehistory, he gave 4,458 as the total of megalithic monuments in France. This figure included many doubtful and destroyed monuments but also did not include many sites which have been discovered and described since his time. At the present day a figure of somewhere between five and five and a half thousand might be the correct one for the megalithic tombs of France. But these quantitative details do not really affect our picture of the French megaliths; at the present day, almost half a century after Déchelette, the distribution pattern of the great French stone-chamber tombs is much the same as he described it, or for that matter as it was mapped by Adrien de Mortillet in 1901.

De Mortillet's map emphasized the fact that the French chamber tombs occur mainly along a line from Brittany to Languedoc, with a less intensive distribution along the foothills of the Pyrenees and extending up the Loire and into Normandy and the Paris Basin. Along the Brittany–Languedoc line, a line which has Brest at one end and Montpellier at the other, there are two areas where chamber tombs are very common; the first is Brittany itself and particularly the departments of Morbihan and Finistère, and the second is the Languedoc and the departments of Aveyron, Ardèche, Lot, Gard, Lozère, and Hérault. In the inventories of megaliths prepared by Déchelette and earlier writers back to Bertrand, the department of the Aveyron was the one with most chamber tombs – it certainly has well over 500, whereas the Morbihan comes fourth with between 300 and 350. Despite this it is the Morbihan which most English readers think of when they think of French megaliths, nor is this a mistake; the concentration of megalithic tombs around Carnac in the south of the Morbihan, and stretching from Carnac to the islands and shores of the little sea which gives its name to the department, is one of the most remarkable collection of chamber tombs in Europe. For variety of form and magnificence of construction these south Morbihan tombs challenge comparison with the great south Spanish tombs; Carnac has been described as a prehistoric metropolis, and there is no doubt that the whole south Morbihan area was one of the greatest importance in the spread of the chamber-tomb builders to France.

Our appreciation of the splendid flourishing of the culture of the megalith builders in the Morbihan and in Brittany generally must not blind us to the chamber tombs elsewhere in France – the great galleries of the Loire valley, for example, or the galleries and rock-cut tombs of the Paris Basin, or to the fact that the six departments now forming the old province of Languedoc between them have more chamber tombs than the whole of the British Isles. There are two notable areas in France without any chamber tombs; one is the Landes country of south-western France, and the other is the Rhône–Saône valley from the Ardèche northwards to eastern France generally.

In France it is not only convenient from the point of view of description, but essential to the understanding of the French collective tombs to distinguish between the passage graves or *dolmens à galerie* as they are called in the French literature and the gallery graves (or *allées couvertes*). The passage graves occur in two quite separate areas, the first in the south-east of France and the second in the north-west; the gallery graves on the other hand are widespread over France – they and the single rectangular chambers occur in most areas where there are megalithic tombs in France. The gallery graves are essentially an inland distribution, or rather they are not obviously in any way concentrated on the seaways; the passage graves on the other hand are essentially a maritime distribution – indeed, I know of no passage grave, or any passage grave in the classic sense we have been using the term in this book, which is more than thirty miles from the sea. There is one other general distinction between the two groups in

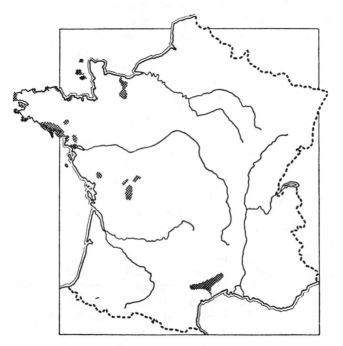

Fig. 15 – Distribution of passage graves in France

France; the passage graves are mainly in round mounds, the gallery graves – while often without any mounds at all – often have long barrows. This is not to say that some passage graves, like Mané Lud or Motte de la Garde or Barnenez, are not set in long barrows (Fig. 15).

The south-east French passage graves occur in one small

97

area extending inland from Frontignan, between Sète and Montpellier, up into the mountains of the Hérault. Frontignan itself has a passage grave, and this site has been known of for seventy-five years; so has the curious passage grave of Collorgues near Uzès in the Rhône Valley some fifty miles north-east of Frontignan. The Collorgues passage grave is now destroyed, but it seems to have been a corbelled tomb and contained apparently a collection of skeletons arranged radially, if contemporary accounts can be believed. In recent years Dr Jean Arnal of Tréviers near Montpellier has studied the Languedocian passage graves in detail and filled in the picture provided by Frontignan and Collorgues. The full extent of this small group is from the coast of Hérault up to the Aveyron border; most of the sites have dry-walled passages leading to rectangular chambers often preceded by a square antechamber : there are frequent portholes and the mounds are invariably circular. The grave-goods from these Hérault passage graves are fairly consistent and comprise leaf-shaped points or spearheads (often notched), arrow-heads, and beads, including the bilobate or winged bead called by French archaeologists *perles à aillettes*. One of the finest and most typical of these sites is Lamalou. Arnal thinks that the Hérault passage-grave builders were searching for the copper and lead of the Aveyron, Hérault, and Gard, and indeed, as from their form and grave-goods they have affinities with the chamber-tomb builders of south-east Spain, we may well suppose them an offshoot of the Millaran folk. It is strange, if they were looking for metal, that there is no metal in their tombs, but that is one of the curious features we shall meet in our study of the much more important passage-grave builders of north-western France and of the British Isles.

One of the most curious features about the tomb of Collorgues is that it contained in it, used as roofing slabs, two megaliths carved with figures of a type well known in southern France. Two of these figures are seen here (Fig. 16) with their stylized treatment of eyes and nose, necklace, and curious object variously described as a sheaf of corn, a hockey-stick, or a hafted axe. In general these figures remind one of some of the representations met with on Iberian chamber tombs, and are like the so-called statue

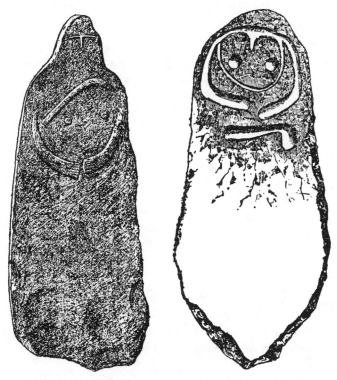

Fig. 16 – Two carved stone figures from Collorgues, Gard

menhirs of southern France. In fact, it seems likely that the Collorgues slabs are two statue-menhirs which have been used in the construction of the tomb. Apart from this the statue-menhirs do not occur in chamber tombs, and, although they are obviously part of the Chalcolithic religious ideas of southern France and, as such, part of the general Chalcolithic culture-complex of Iberia, do not coincide with the passage graves or gallery graves of southern

France. They stand alone in Aveyron and Tarn and the southern Rhône, with a curiously restricted distribution. They look, like the passage graves, back to the east Mediterranean, but through a different channel of culture transmission from that of the passage graves.

In north-western France passage graves occur most notably in the southern Morbihan region centred around Carnac, Auray, and Vannes; this is classically the home of the famous Breton passage graves, and here we get dry-walled monuments with corbelled roofs like Île Longue which could with no surprise have been found in the Los Millares or Alcalá cemetery, and also megalithic passage graves like Kercado and many another, which would have been in place in the megalithic passage-grave cemeteries of central Portugal. There are no rock-cut passage graves in Brittany. Apart from this central area of distribution there are small groups of passage graves down the coast of the Bay of Biscay as far as the Charente, and along to southwest Finistère, and small pockets along the north coast of Brittany as far as St Malo. One or two passage graves occur in Normandy, including the remarkable site of Fontenay-le-Marmion, near Caen in Calvados, where no less than twelve passage graves were set in a single round mound 130 feet in diameter. The Channel Islands should also be included in this list of passage graves in north-western France; both Jersey and Guernsey contain good examples of passage graves (Fig. 17).

The grave-goods from the north-west French passage graves and especially the classic ones of the Morbihan are many and varied; undecorated pottery like that found in the Iberian passage graves is common and decorated pottery of the Chassey style as well as beakers. Leaf-shaped arrow-heads occur though rarely; transverse and barbed and tanged flint arrow-heads are most common. No copper axes or daggers or, for that matter, copper or bronze tools and weapons of any kind have been found in Breton passage graves; the industry is lithic and includes polished stone axes. There often occur in the tombs large, thin, and

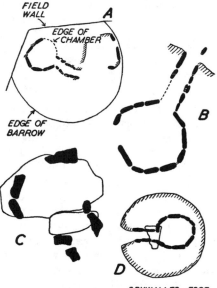

FIELD WALL

A

EDGE OF CHAMBER

EDGE OF BARROW

B

C

D

DRYWALLED EDGE OF BARROW

Fig. 17 – Typical Breton passage graves

(A) Brunec, Finistère
(B) Bazognes-en-Pareds, Vendée
(C) Le Blanchot, Loire Atlantique
(D) Parc Guren, Morbihan

superbly made polished axes of fibrolite and greenstone; these do not seem to have been used. Some of them have expanded blades as though they were imitating copper axes. There are also double axes of stone, clearly imitating the Minoan metal double-axe. Indeed, it seems most likely that the fine stonework found in the Breton passage graves is a kind of substitute for metalwork. In the absence of literary evidence the archaeologist can only guess at what this substitution means. If, as seems likely, the builders of the Breton passage graves were prospectors looking for copper and other valuable stones and ores, metal objects may have assumed a special importance for them. They may have traded metal ores away back to the Mediterranean while they themselves, for some reasons we cannot precisely apprehend, never placed copper and bronze objects in their tombs, but instead, stone copies of them. These are archaeological facts easier to describe than explain.

Certainly the fine polished stone axes were one of the splendid features of the industry of the Breton tomb builders and were carried to Britain and to Portugal. There are hardly any cult objects in the Breton passage graves comparable with those found in Iberia; we find no schist plaques and no idols in Brittany, but the little pot from Er-Mar is really in the tradition of the south Iberian idols whereas much of the channelled ornament of the pottery is surely to be derived from the *symbolkeramik* of Iberia. The Breton passage graves contain beads of talc, callais, rock-crystal, and gold, and axe-amulets and bracelets of hammered gold. Callais is an imperfect form of turquoise; and beads of it are also found in south Portugal and in southern France. It may well be that callais and gold were worked locally in the Morbihan and traded back along the western routes to Iberia and southern France.

We have already said that while the French passage graves are restricted in their distribution, the gallery graves and the single rectangular chambers are much more widespread. We can here refer to some only of the groups of gallery graves. One of the most famous is near Arles, actually between Arles and Fontvieille in Bouches-du-Rhône. Here, on what must have been in the first half of the second millennium an island, are four rock-cut tombs and one surface megalithic tomb, which are collectively known in archaeological literature as the Arles *grottes*. The Grottes des Fées (or the Épée de Roland) is the most famous; it consists of a long gallery 75 feet long by about 10 feet broad, cut in the rock, with six steps leading down into it and two side-chambers opening off the entrance to the gallery. It has been known of for a very long time and no scientific excavation of this site has been possible. Another of the four rock-cut sites, the Grotte du Castellet, was dug in 1876 and produced the remains of 100 inhumęd skeletons, 33 arrow-heads of flint (one of which was stuck in the vertebrae of one of the skeletons), 114 callais beads, one gold head, a plaque of gold, and beakers.

Another very important group of gallery graves occurs along the Carcassonne Gap between Narbonne and Toulouse; these monuments, not so well known to English readers as the Arles *grottes*, comprise galleries such as Boun-Marcou, Jappeloup, St Eugène, and le Palet de Roland. St Eugène, near Carcassonne, contained 300 interments, seven beakers, twelve palettes, gold and callais beads, and tanged arrow-heads. There are also gallery graves in the foot-hills of the Pyrenees; those of La Halliade and Taillan have been long known in archaeological literature. The Pyrenean foot-hills also contain numbers of single rectangular chambers, and the great numbers of chamber tombs in the Aveyron, Tarn, and Lozère – concentrated as they are on the *causses* country of the Languedoc – are mainly single rectangular chambers and short galleries. Many of these are set in long mounds. Some of the burial chambers on the *causses* country of the Languedoc carry on the tradition of megalithic tomb building to a period much later than that of the fine galleries we have been describing. In some of the Aveyron tombs have been found copper daggers and pins characteristic of the Early Bronze Age, and indeed there seems little doubt that some of these tombs were being used, and some probably constructed, right on into the last quarter of the second millennium B.C. It seems likely that the great numbers of chamber tombs on the *causses* is due to an entirely different reason from the great numbers in the Morbihan; in the Morbihan the megalithic culture is rich and flourishing from the beginning, in the *causses* it looks like a culture which lingered on for a very long time – perhaps until after 1000 B.C.

There are certain features in some of these south French galleries which are of particular interest to students of chambered tombs in the British Isles. Portholes occur quite commonly in the rock-cut tombs at Arles and in the Carcassonne-gap galleries, and some of the tombs, like St Eugène itself and La Halliade, are segmented. Both these features occur sporadically in the British galleries. Marked forecourts with horns are missing in the south French galleries, although a group of slightly .later tombs in Hérault and Gard have forecourts. The origin of the south French galleries is distributionally not difficult to seek; we may picture settlers arriving by sea, building their tombs on an island near Arles and along the foot-hills of the Carcassonne Gap. At first these tombs were rock-cut, and then, it is suggested, surface megalithic versions of them were constructed which, probably for constructional reasons, needed a covering or supporting mound of earth and stones. These mounds, not unnaturally, took the shape of the long tombs, and so, long barrows or cairns came into existence. We suggest, then, that the megalithic tombs, properly speaking, of south France are a translation into megalithic architecture of the rock-cut tombs in much the same way as the megalithic monuments of Iberia are translations of the dry-walled tombs. Where the original settlers came from is a more difficult question to answer; the Balearics, Sardinia, and south Spain have all been suggested, and are all possibilities. Certainly some of the Balearic rock-cut tombs compare closely with the Arles *grottes*, even to the extent of having side-chambers, and we have already noticed the curious elongated mound above the tomb at Son Caulellas. On the other hand it may be that the Arles settlers are only a slightly different group from those who landed at Frontignan and built the Hérault passage graves.

We have hitherto been talking about the gallery graves of southern France; north of the Garonne there are gallery graves in Angoumois, Poitou, up the lower Loire, and in Brittany and Normandy. Some of these, like the monuments at Saumur, or the great gallery grave of Essé, near Rennes, are so large and remarkable that one wonders whether, free-standing as they are at the present day, they were ever covered by mounds. In Brittany there is a marked difference in the distribution of gallery graves and passage graves; the gallery graves are widespread and occur inland as well as along the sea coast. This does not mean that their distribution is mutually exclusive; far from it – and in the classic area of Carnac–Vannes we find both gallery graves and passage graves and there is really no possibility of distinguishing between them in time. The gallery graves of the Morbihan contain much the same grave-goods as the passage graves with one notable exception; the gallery graves have, much more than the passage graves, a coarse, flat-bottomed type of pottery, often looking like a flowerpot, that is often referred to in archaeological literature as Seine–Oise–Marne pottery or Horgen ware. We shall discuss this pottery in a moment. Here we are concerned only with the Morbihan tombs. A remarkable flowering of megalithic architecture took place in the Morbihan and all sorts of variant types of tombs were invented. One type usually referred to by the French as the *allée couverte coudée* (and in English as the 'bent gallery grave') is more likely to be a variant of the standard passage grave; another, which has been described by the present writer as the 'transepted gallery grave', may well have passage-grave heritage in its make-up. These precise typological and archaeological questions should not obtrude on the general picture which is one of a variety of funerary traditions which interacted on each other. Some of these traditions are not collective and megalithic; there are burials in unchambered long barrows in Brittany and in unchambered round barrows and both are perhaps earlier than the first collective tombs. Then, as we have seen, there are collective burials in passage graves and gallery graves and later in closed tombs like St Michel which are local Breton developments. It is not, therefore, surprising that in south Brittany there should develop a number of non-funerary megalithic monuments – the great stone avenues – which are without parallel in western Europe.

The Megalith Builders of Western Europe

The living sites of the Morbihan folk are, as always with megalith builders, less well known than their tombs, but at sites like the Camp de Lizo, near Carnac – a small promontory fort – we certainly have one of their settlement sites. One of the pots from Le Lizo has a decoration resembling the owl-face or *oculi* motif so common in Iberia, and we must mention here, though it is not in Brittany, settlement sites like the Camp de Peu Richard near Saintes, in the Charente-Maritime. This settlement site has yielded pottery with more precisely-defined owl or *oculi* motifs, and this kind of pottery, obviously derived from the Iberian *symbolkeramik*, but unassociated at Peu Richard with collective tombs, shows how we must not look at the spread of Chalcolithic culture through western Europe too rigidly in terms of a single trait, or for that matter, expect a linked series of traits to appear everywhere. It is reasonably beyond question that the builders of the Breton passage graves were settlers from south Spain and Portugal; and it is equally clear that the settlers at Peu Richard, with their *oculi*-ornamented pottery, come from the same Chalcolithic contexts in southern Iberia.

It is the same sort of problem and solution as we hinted at in discussing the statue-menhirs and megalithic tombs of southern France. We cannot draw our categories too sharply, and in France, as elsewhere in western Europe, any discussion that begins with chamber tombs must spread on to non-megalithic contexts. The reverse of the distinction between decorated non-funerary monuments (the statue-menhirs) and undecorated funerary monuments which occurs in south France, occurs in the Morbihan. Here, as in megalithic architecture, there is a great flowering of megalithic art, and it is confined almost entirely to the passage graves – if we include with them, as we should on formal grounds, the angled passage graves like Les Pierres Plates, etc., which the French archaeologists call *allées couvertes coudées*. The art is confined to a small number of tombs in the Carnac area, and extends westwards to south Finistère; it is all engraved, or rather pocked, and at first sight has no immediate connexion with the art on the Iberian passage graves. Some of the designs rather look like statue-menhirs; others with zigzag lines, spirals, concentric circles, and half-circles do go back to some of the Iberian designs. The Breton megalithic art

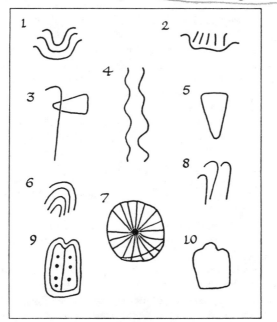

Fig. 18 – Some characteristic symbols occurring in south Breton megalithic art

(1) The *yoke* symbol
(2) The *ship* symbol
(3) Hafted axe
(4) Zigzag lines (snakes?)
(5) Axehead
(6) Concentric half-elipses
(7) Rayed circle, wheel, or *sun* symbol
(8) The *crook* motif
(9) Stylized human figure
(10) The *buckler* or *petit marmite* symbol

probably drew inspiration from two sources – the Chalcolithic traditions of Iberia and south France – and that may account for its vigour and freshness. Gavrinnis is one of the most remarkable decorated tombs in the whole of western Europe (Fig. 18).

The Megalith Builders of Western Europe

One group of north French gallery graves remains to be described; these are situated in the Paris Basin along the river valley of the Seine from east of Rouen to Paris itself, and up the tributaries of the Epte, Eure, Aisne, Oise, and Marne. Most of these gallery graves are set in the sides of hills; many of them have marked portals or portal chambers with a septal slab marking off the rest of the chamber, and many have portholes. At least five of these gallery graves have carved figures at the entrance to the tomb and these figures are without doubt the goddess-figure which appeared in the Iberian cult objects and tombs and in a different guise on the statue-menhirs of southern France. In the soft chalk of the Upper Marne and Petit Morin valleys, these tombs are entirely rock-cut, and in four of these – there are about a hundred of the rock-cut tombs – the funerary goddess figure is extremely well represented. The normal grave furniture of this Paris Basin group consists of polished flint axes normally mounted in perforated sleeves of antler, antler axes, daggers of the flint from Grand Pressigny in Touraine, transverse arrow-heads, and coarse splay-footed flower-pots such as we have mentioned came from some of the Breton gallery graves. The ornaments include shells, rings, and arc-pendants of stone, axe-amulets and amulets made out of pieces of skull. Quite a number of the skulls in the Paris Basin galleries have been trephined. A few sherds of beaker from the Paris galleries of Bennemont show that they began at a time contemporary with the main *floruit* of the megalith builders, but the occurrence of flanged axes of bronze from some of these galleries shows that the Paris galleries, like the galleries and simple chambers of the *causses* country, went on into the last quarter of the second millennium B.C. Bosch Gimpera invented the term 'Seine–Oise–Marne culture' for the culture of the Paris Basin megalith builders, and in archaeological literature there is much talk of Seine–Oise–Marne, or S.O.M., galleries and of S.O.M. pots. This is not a very good nomenclature; the splay-footed flower-pots labelled S.O.M. occur in non-megalithic contexts in western France as well as Switzerland, in which latter country they are called Horgen ware. We must think of the megalith builders in the Paris Basin as intruding on a population which was epi-Mesolithic, a population of hunting–fishing barbarians who had learnt some of the arts associated with the Neolithic, but who were practising those arts, like potting, in a very clumsy way. The material culture of these megalith builders in the Paris Basin is partly that of the indigenous natives and partly what they brought in from outside.

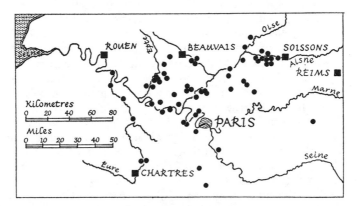

Fig. 19 – Distribution of megalithic gallery graves in the Paris Basin

From what outside direction did these megalith builders come? Professor Gordon Childe argued that they came from southern France and emphasized the local imitation of the Egyptian–early Aegean leg amulet, the tomb plans, the sculptures, and the trephined skulls. At one time it seemed to the present writer that the Paris galleries were the result of a spread up the Loire, but now it seems more likely that the megalith builders came up the Seine. The distribution is essentially one that suggests river penetration, and this may well be part of a general, initially coastal, settlement of north-western France by the builders of gallery graves. But where, then, did the gallery graves of western France come from? This is a wider and more difficult question. Some, believing in the south French origin of the Paris Basin gallery graves, would see all the north-west French gallery graves as an extension of the Paris Basin tombs. This is a working hypothesis, but it will only work if we can show that the Breton and Channel Islands gallery graves are later than the earliest Paris Basin gallery graves. Some of the Breton gallery graves have yielded material which certainly makes them contemporary or later than the Paris galleries, but some have yielded Chalcolithic material – beakers in particular – and western Neolithic pottery which suggests that some of the Breton gallery graves were in use long before the Paris Basin galleries. In view of this, and the chronological evidence we have for the date of the south French gallery graves, and for the Severn–Cotswold tombs (almost certainly to be derived from the Breton gallery graves) it seems likely that the west French gallery graves come from southern France via the Narbonne–Corbilo route which was so important in later French history. It is quite true that the great concentration of French megaliths is along the line from Languedoc to Brittany, as we stressed at the outset of this chapter.

Nevertheless, it now seems likely that while there may be a long component in the north French gallery graves that comes along the Narbonne–Corbilo route, the main component is a sea-borne one settling at various points along the north-west and north French coast, and one which comes essentially from southern Iberia. The distribution of the goddess figure on the north French gallery graves so clearly reminiscent of the Dolmen de Soto, seems by itself to argue this.

The more one studies the French collective tombs – as indeed French prehistory as a whole – it becomes clear that there was in prehistoric France constantly a dual relationship with the Mediterranean homeland of culture: one which affected the south-east of France, and another along the Atlantic highways which affected western and

northern France. These two routes were probably responsible for the two groups of passage graves and also probably for the gallery graves. They need not, of course, be
very different in date. Yet somehow there was probably
some difference in culture. The passage graves from their
distribution suggest intrusive folk looking probably for
metal and precious objects. The gallery graves and associated single rectangular chambers which go on so much
longer, suggest that this tomb form was taken over by the
indigenes of France. Dr Gabrielle Fabre has emphasized
that the megalith builders of the Pyrenean region, which
she has been studying, were pastoralists; the grave-goods
of the Paris gallery-grave builders, according to Childe,
'disclose a warlike population living by stock-breeding and
hunting, but almost certainly also tilling the soil'.[1] It
would be a false simplification to see a duality in French
prehistory between passage-grave metal prospectors and
gallery-grave pastoralists, but such a false oversimplification may yet help to pin down the idea we are trying to
convey here, namely that the passage graves probably
represent the earliest megalith settlers in France, fresh
from their Chalcolithic homes in Iberia, looking for metal
and precious stones, whereas the gallery graves were tombs
of perhaps slightly later settlers from the same areas who
mixed more with the natives and whose tomb forms were
widely adopted. Why was this? Was it because the house-
of-cards architecture of Saumur and the Paris gallery graves
was easier to do than the corbelled vaults of Île Longue?
It may well be so, but we shall never know.

1. *The Dawn of European Civilization*, 1957, p. 313.

6

THE BRITISH ISLES

THERE are at the present day something between fifteen hundred and two thousand megalithic tombs in the British Isles. Their distribution is essentially western and north-western; at the present day England and Wales between them probably have no more than two hundred and fifty megalithic tombs, Scotland perhaps three hundred and fifty, and Ireland getting on for a thousand or more. From detailed studies of various areas of the British Isles as samples, it may well be that the original number of megalithic tombs constructed in these islands was in the neighbourhood of three to four thousand. Most of the tombs surviving at the present day are in coastal areas and islands – the Orkneys, Shetlands, and the Isles of Scilly are rich in these tombs – with the exception of Ireland where there are great penetrations inland. Indeed, those two facts seem the key to the geographical distribution of the British collective tombs – coastal settlements and then penetrations inland, up river valleys, or into suitable hilly country like the Cotswolds and the north Wiltshire downs.

Throughout the emphasis distributionally is on the western seaways, with one exception. There is a very small group of megalithic tombs in the Medway valley of Kent – no more than three or four tombs between Rochester and Maidstone, of which Kit's Coty House has become famous because of its accessibility. These sites are rectangular chambers set in rectangular barrows, and although other suggestions have been made, they look like extensions to England of the 'dolmens' of northern Europe. There is really nothing but their form and construction to go on, but these Medway tombs may well be members of the

dös/dysse class of the Danish Neolithic. These monuments
which, we have argued, started in Danish Early Neolithic
C in south Jutland, spread in the Middle Neolithic into
northern Germany and north-eastern Holland. They may,
at the same time, have spread to Kent. Certainly other
archaeological evidence of contact between eastern England and Denmark exists at this period.

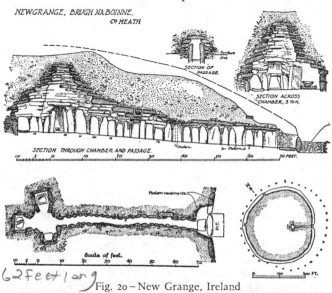

62 feet long

Fig. 20 – New Grange, Ireland

But apart from the Medway group our British megalithic tombs are keyed distributionally, and, as we shall
see, morphologically to France and Iberia. Ireland has a
fine collection of passage graves whose distribution was
studied some years ago by T. G. E. Powell; he distinguished
a Dublin Group, a Boyne Group, an Armagh Group, a north
Antrim Group, as well as some scattered sites; it is now
quite common to refer to all the Irish passage graves as
belonging to the Boyne Culture. Some of them are very
fine monuments indeed; New Grange consists of a passage
62 feet long leading to a chamber roofed with a wonderful

corbelled vault, the top of which is nearly 20 feet from the floor, the whole standing in a round mound 265 feet in diameter and about 45 feet high (Fig. 20). Many of the Irish passage graves, like New Grange, Knowth, and Dowth on the River Boyne, are grouped in cemeteries, like Alcalá and the groups of cemeteries in the Carnac–Locmariaquer area. On the Lochcrew Hills in County Meath stood a cemetery of about thirty chambered tombs; Carrowkeel Mountain, in Sligo, has a cemetery of fourteen tombs and Carrowmore about sixty.

Among all these Irish passage graves there is very considerable variety of plan; Tibradden is a classic west European passage grave with a round, dry-walled, originally corbelled roof chamber; New Grange, while classic in construction, has a very long passage and a central chamber with three side-chambers opening out of it – this so-called Irish cruciform passage grave plan is well represented at Lochcrew and Carrowkeel, and in both these cemeteries there are monuments in which the cruciform idea is breaking down into more complicated and local variants (e.g. Lochcrew L and Carrowkeel F). In the Carrowmore cemetery of chamber tombs the tombs are megalithic in construction. The barrows of the Boyne Culture tombs are round. The burial rite in these tombs seems to have been mainly cremation; the grave-goods are slight, consisting of a coarse decorated ware called Lochcrew ware, pins and needles of bone or antler, stone beads and pendants, including pestle or mace-head-shaped pendants.

New Grange itself is one of a group of chambered barrows forming a cemetery on the River Boyne. Three of these tombs – New Grange itself, Dowth, and Knowth have elaborate ornament on walling and roofing stones; the great stone across the entrance to the passage at New Grange, with its splendidly executed and highly stylized pattern of spirals and lozenges, is one of the best-known examples of megalithic mural art. There are several decorated tombs in the Lochcrew cemetery and about half a dozen more examples of mural megalithic art among the

Boyne culture tombs. The motifs represented are many –
spirals, triangles, zigzag lines, circles, lozenges, and some of
these designs seem purely geometrical. There are, however,
unmistakable *oculi* designs recalling the goddess figure of
Chalcolithic France, Iberia, and the west Mediterranean
(e.g. the roofing stone of the north side-chamber at New
Grange, or Knockmany), and many of the apparently geometrical designs may really be stylized representations of
a goddess figure.

From their form and their mural art the Boyne tombs
must surely represent a settlement, probably in eastern
Ireland, of people from western France or western Iberia.
Parallels to the art exist in Brittany and Iberia and the idea
of a cruciform passage grave seems to be crystallizing, for
example, in the Alcalá cemetery of south Portugal. This
movement along the western seaways to Ireland might
well have taken place in the early years of the second
millennium B.C. and it is noteworthy that there are no
beakers in the Irish passage graves. We have seen that the
Iberian evidence suggests that megalithic architecture had
a long life, and it seems likely that the Boyne Culture
flourished in Ireland at least for half a millennium. At
Carrowkeel two food vessels of British Middle Bronze Age
type were deposited in the chamber tombs in circumstances which suggest a late moment in the primary collective use of tombs; the pestle-shaped pendants can be
paralleled in amber in the Wessex Culture of the British
Early Bronze Age (usually dated from 1700 to 1300 B.C.);
and it is difficult not to see a synchronism between the art
of the entrance stone and some other slabs at New Grange
with the mural megalithic art of Malta and Castelluccio
and eventually the shaft graves of Mycenae. It would seem
reasonable then, at present to say that while the first Irish
passage graves might have been built somewhere between
2000 and 1800 B.C. a monument like New Grange itself
might have been constructed (or at least decorated) at 1500
B.C. and local developments of the Boyne tombs were being
constructed or used during the next half-millennium.

The Megalith Builders of Western Europe

Many of the Irish chambered tombs were re-used at a later date as shelters or metal workshops, and the nineteenth-century excavations of Lochcrew H produced engraved bone objects of the Celtic La Tène style of the late first millennium B.C., which have until recently been interpreted as proving the use of this disused tomb as the atelier of a Celtic artist of that time (the Irish Early Iron Age). In 1943 this monument was re-excavated by Dr Joseph Raftery, who claims to have shown that it was 'erected in the Early Iron Age, and used exclusively as a burial place', and that 'Cruciform passage graves, assuming an Early Bronze Age date for their inception, continued for a long time with little radical change of plan'.[1]

The Boyne Culture folk spread across the Irish Sea to west Wales where the passage graves of Bryn Celli Ddu and Barclodiad y Gawres attest their settlements in Anglesey, and the Calderstones a settlement at Liverpool. All these three sites have mural megalithic art and Barclodiad y Gawres is a cruciform passage grave. They also spread up the west coast of Scotland to the Hebrides, to Cromarty, and to the Orkneys, where Maes Howe is one of the most splendid examples of our British passage graves – an entrance passage 36 feet long leads into a squared version of the cruciform plan, 15 feet square, all set in a round mound 115 feet in diameter and 24 feet high (Fig. 21). On the south side of the Moray Firth is a group of some thirty chambered tombs usually referred to as the Clava Group; they are passage graves and the best of them are classic in

1. Raftery, *Prehistoric Ireland*, 1951, p. 106. It seems surprising but is not, of course, impossible that passage graves should have been built in Ireland for two thousand years. As I write, the full account of Raftery's re-excavation of Lochcrew H is not available. It is certainly odd that, if Raftery's conclusions are right, there should be contemporary at one site two entirely different art styles; mobiliary art of the La Tène period, and mural art of the Chalcolithic. It is, of course, possible that stones decorated in a style of the second millennium B.C., and originally part of a megalithic tomb, were re-used in a later monument. Let us not forget that there were stone tombs rather like passage graves constructed in Iberia and Denmark in the first millennium.

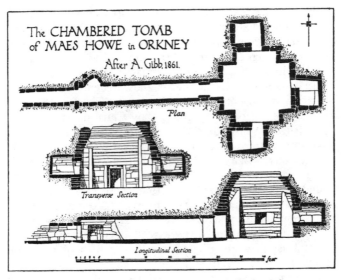

Fig. 21 – Plan and section of Maes Howe in the Orkneys

form and in construction, with corbelled vaults springing from a wall of orthostats and dry-walling behind. They are strikingly like the early monuments in Iberia, western France, and Ireland, and, at least on formal and constructional grounds, ought to represent an early settlement on the shores of the Moray Firth. Did the first pioneer passage-grave settlers coming up the Irish Sea go all round the north of Scotland to Clava as well, or did some of the pioneers who, we have suggested, went through the English Channel on their way to Denmark, sail up the eastern coast of England and Scotland until they got so far north? We cannot produce the answer; either way it seems puzzling, but perhaps less so if we bear in mind that some early navigators must have made the journey from – to put it at its shortest – the Channel Islands to Sylt, and that must have been more than six hundred miles – if the Danish passage graves are to be derived from the west.

A small group of that specialized type of passage grave

called an 'entrance grave' exists in south-eastern Ireland and the south-west of Cornwall, and especially the Isles of Scilly. This group has been called the Scilly–Tramore group, and from the plans of the tombs and their distribution they look like a settlement of late passage-grave people from Finistère or the Channel Islands. Recently, precise information has become available about their date. Faience and glass beads found at Knackyboy Cairn on St Martin's, in the Isles of Scilly, date the use of one of these entrance graves probably over several centuries down to about 1000 B.C.; at Harristown, in County Waterford, faience beads of the same date were secondary to the construction of the mound. It seems, then, likely that these entrance graves were being constructed between, say, 1500 and 1000 B.C. It still remains a mystery why so many of them occur in the Isles of Scilly, where there still survive to the present day at least fifty chambered tombs – a fifth of the total number in England and Wales.

Let us now move from monuments obviously in the passage-grave tradition to monuments which, whatever their ultimate origins, do not at the present day immediately fit into the passage-grave tradition. The first group is to be found in South Wales and the south-west Midlands, and is generally referred to as the Severn–Cotswold group. It consists of long barrows, some of which have false or dummy entrances at their broader ends and the burial chambers set laterally in the mound (e.g. Belas Knap and Rodmarton) but most of which have the burial chamber set at the broad end approached by a cuspate or V-shaped forecourt. The usual form of chamber is the gallery grave (e.g. Heston Brake) or a large rectangular chamber (e.g. Tinkinswood) or the transepted gallery grave consisting of one, two, or more pairs of transepts set off the main gallery. The barrow varies in size from 60 feet in length to great monuments like East Kennet and West Kennet in north Wiltshire, which are nearly 350 feet in length. Here, as at New Grange, the barrow itself has attained a size disproportionate to its necessity as a revetting and covering

mound for a tomb. It is not possible in a subject so fraught
with uncertainties and controversies as is the study of
megalithic tombs to lay down any laws about the evolution of this unusual and early form of European architecture, but it would seem that when the mounds become
extraordinarily large and out of all proportion to their
basic function, as they are at Bougon or St Michel or as are
New Grange and the Kennet long barrows, we are well
away from the basic common traditions that the megalith
tomb builders first diffused. The grave-goods in the Severn–
Cotswold tombs consist of undecorated western Neolithic
pottery, leaf-shaped arrow-heads, stone discs, bone chisels,
and shale beads. There is evidence of Peterborough and
beaker ware in secondary associations in the Severn–Cotswold tombs, and in 1955, in their re-excavation of the West
Kennet long barrow, Piggott and Atkinson found in the
filling of the transeptal chambers, whose presence had been
missed by Thurnam the nineteenth-century excavator,
stratigraphical proof that the early use of West Kennet was
before the arrival of the Beaker Folk in southern Britain.
Indeed, some of the material from the early use of West
Kennet is so like some material from the neighbouring
settlement of Windmill Hill (which has given its name to
the first British Neolithic culture, the non-megalithic Windmill Hill culture characterized by causewayed camps and
earthen long barrows) that we must put the beginnings of
the Severn–Cotswold megalith builders as quite early in
the British Neolithic. Piggott in his *Neolithic Cultures of
the British Isles* (1954) would date the Windmill Hill culture as beginning soon after 2000 B.C. and the chambered
tombs of the Severn–Cotswold culture perhaps a century
later. It seems to me likely that the Windmill Hill culture
may have spread to southern England before 2000 B.C. and
the Severn–Cotswold tombs should be dated somewhere
between 2000 and 1700 B.C.

From the distributional pattern of the Severn–Cotswold
tombs as a whole, and the earlier terminally chambered
tombs especially, it is clear they represent a settlement on

the shores of the Bristol Channel. Whence came these settlers? Ireland has been suggested and it is certainly true that the developed cruciform passage grave could, on for-

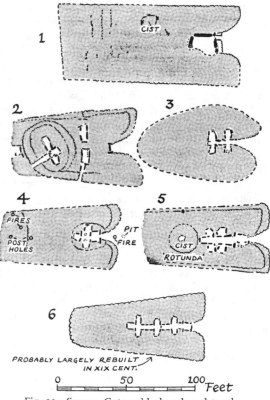

Fig. 22 – Severn–Cotswold chambered tombs

(1) Tinkinswood, Glamorgan	(4) Nympsfield, Gloucestershire
(2) Ty Isaf, Brecknockshire	(5) Notgrove, Gloucestershire
(3) Parc le Breos Cwm, Glamorgan	(6) Stoney Littleton, Somerset

mal grounds alone, be argued as the parent of the transepted gallery grave. The most likely area, however, is the west coast of France, particularly the area between the Vendée and the Morbihan, where there occur all the types of monument found in the terminally chambered long barrows of the Severn–Cotswold group – gallery graves, transepted gallery graves, and large rectangular chambers. We must most probably envisage a movement of people from the south-east of Brittany and the Lower Loire to the Severn Sea soon after 2000 B.C.

In another more northern part of the British Isles, northern Ireland and south-west Scotland, with outliers in the Isle of Man and west Wales, there occur more megalithic tombs with many resemblances to some of the Severn–Cotswold tombs. These tombs are usually grouped together and called the Clyde–Carlingford Group and their characteristic form of megalithic tomb conceived of as an oval or wedge-shaped cairn usually 70 to 80 feet long by 40 to 50 feet wide with a long rectangular gallery normally segmented into two or three or more chambers opening on to the wider of the two narrow ends of the barrow and recessed in that end by means of a forecourt often semicircular in shape. Good examples of this type of tomb in south-west Scotland are Carn Ban in Arran and Cairn Holy in Galloway; typical northern Irish examples are Ballyalton, Goward, and Clady Halliday. The grave-goods in these tombs include much western Neolithic ware including unornamented, shouldered, round-bottomed bowls which Piggott now proposes to call Lyles Hill ware, and bowls ornamented with channelled decoration usually referred to as Beacharra ware (or Beacharra B in Piggott's new classification), other pottery decorated with impressed, twisted, or whipped cord techniques referred to as Sandhills or Beacharra C ware, and fourthly, coarse flat-bottomed ware which for a while the early excavators of these north Irish tombs thought was intrusive Early Iron Age or Late Bronze Age ware. Other grave-goods include leaf- and lozenge-shaped arrow-heads and polished stone axes, including three of porcellanite from the axe factory of Tievebulliagh, and one at Cairn Holy I of pyroxene jadeite from Brittany.

Within the Clyde–Carlingford area of south-west

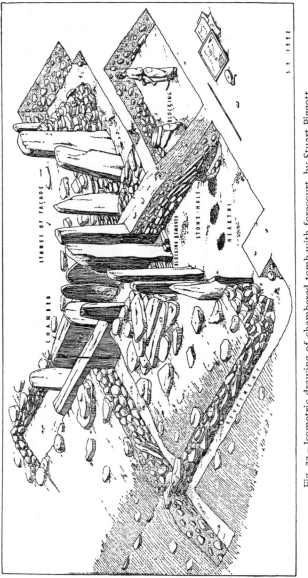

Fig. 23 – Isometric drawing of chambered tomb with forecourt, by Stuart Piggott

Scotland there is a considerable variety of tomb-plan which in principle recalls the Cotswold–Severn developments; here too, in Scotland are found laterally chambered barrows and false entrances. In northern Ireland there is great variety in the number of segments in the chambers; and a variety of long barrow called at first by archaeologists 'double-horned cairns' or 'lobster-claw cairns' and for some of which Professor De Valera has now suggested the name 'court cairn'. These monuments which are concentrated in north-western and western Ireland have central unroofed courts and segmented chambers opening out of them. Much has been written and is still being written about the inter-relations of the various types of horned cairns and court cairns in Ireland and south-west Scotland, and the continental affinities of these monuments.

Estyn Evans and Oliver Davies saw the origin of the tombs as a settlement of people in the Carlingford estuary who had come from Sardinia directly by sea. The grave-goods of the Clyde–Carlingford tombs and the local evidence of their pre-beaker date, as well as the evidence for

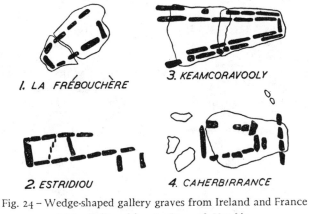

1. LA FRÉBOUCHÈRE

3. KEAMCORAVOOLY

2. ESTRIDIOU

4. CAHERBIRRANCE

Fig. 24 – Wedge-shaped gallery graves from Ireland and France

  (1) La Frébouchère, Le Bernard, Vendée
  (2) Estridiou, Finistère
  (3) Keamcoravooly, County Cork
  (4) Caherbirrance, County Cork

the late date of the Sardinian giants' graves, makes a Sardinian origin most improbable. Yet in south France we find many of the elements that occur in the Clyde–Carlingford tombs, and these elements are found sporadically in north-western France – segmentation, for example, and oval barrows. Beacharra B ware must surely be derived from the channelled ware of southern France. But there are not to the best of my knowledge any semicircular forecourts in western France and no precise parallel to the Irish horned cairns, and it seems most probable to me that this type of megalithic tomb evolved in the British Isles. De Valera has proposed reversing the usual typological sequence, and makes the horned cairn of the Ballyalton–Carn Ban type a development in eastern Ireland of the court cairns of western Ireland, which he argues represent a sea-borne settlement in Mayo and Sligo. He does not tell us where these Mayo–Sligo court cairn builders came from, and there are no real parallels for them outside the British Isles.

While we must certainly allow direct influences from western France up the western seaways to south-west Scotland and north-east Ireland, it seems to me most probable at present that the Clyde–Carlingford tombs are an off-shoot of the Severn–Cotswold tombs, or part of the same movement that produced the Severn–Cotswold tombs. There are other gallery graves in Ireland which may have a more direct contact with western France. It is now customary to distinguish among the three or four hundred Irish gallery graves which do not belong to the horned cairn–court cairn group a northern group of wedge-shaped galleries such as Dunteige and Moylisha and Ballyedmonduff, and a southern group of wedge-shaped galleries such as Labbacallee in County Cork. The form of some of these monuments closely recalls some of the Breton gallery graves, and coarse flat-bottomed pottery such as occurs in the Breton gallery graves occurs in them. Beaker pottery also occurs in several examples; there was a looped spearhead mould from Moylisha, while Loughash yielded fragments of a bronze blade with the principal interment, and a palstave mould allegedly contemporary with the sealing of the cairn. The so-called 'portal dolmens' of Ireland are probably to be connected with some aspects of the development of these wedge-shaped gallery graves.

We cannot here go any further into the complexities of the colonization of the British Isles in the second millennium and before, along the western seaways that then linked Ireland and Scotland and western Britain with

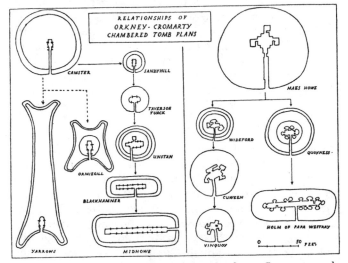

Fig. 25 – Diagram of suggested typology of Orkney–Cromarty tombs
(after Stuart Piggott)

France and Iberia. There were many movements and settlements of people, some of which were unassociated with megalithic tombs. We are just beginning to distinguish a western Neolithic in the British Isles of a non-megalithic facies. From then on we see complicated settlements of tomb builders, the Boyne passage-grave builders from Iberia, the Scilly–Tramore folk from Brittany or the Channel Islands, the Severn–Cotswold and Clyde–Carlingford settlers from western France, and the Irish gallery-

grave builders from Brittany. With these various strains it
is no wonder that in some areas of the British Isles local
varieties of tombs were built which defy any typological
classification and should defy it; northern Scotland and the
Orkneys and Shetlands are one of the areas *par excellence*
in western Europe to demonstrate the local development
of tomb types. Piggott has recently, with very considerable
success, arranged the Orkney–Cromarty chambered tomb
plans in typological sequences going back to passage graves
like Camster and Maes Howe; when we get to monuments
like Midhowe and the Holm of Papa Westray we see how
far local invention has gone. But what is interesting is that
even in the Holm of Papa Westray, with its bizarre plan
unparalleled elsewhere in western Europe there were two
groups of engravings in the style of the Boyne tombs, including an *oculus* motif, taking us back at once from the
remote north of the British Isles to the cult idols of southern Iberia.

Very gradually we are learning about the dwelling-
places of some of these folk who built the chambered
tombs and one of the best known is at Lough Gur in
County Limerick where in round and rectangular houses
Professor ÓRíordáin found a western Neolithic culture
with round-bottomed, undecorated pottery, leaf and
lozenge arrow-heads, and polished stone axes, which gradually is replaced by coarse flat-bottomed ware, and over-
lain by beaker. The Lough Gur people, or some of them,
were buried in a gallery grave near by, and also built a
circular ritual monument. We cannot here do more than
mention the complex problem of the megalithic stone
circles of the British Isles. There is a great variety among
the structures listed as stone circles and henge monuments,
and almost certainly one aspect of the origin of the henge
monument lies in cultures not originally using megalithic
stones. On the other hand, stone circles exist in the western
megalithic areas and as we have seen at Lough Gur are
closely associated with the megalith-tomb builders. I think
we shall not be far from the truth if we see in the great

stone circles of England the result of the acculturation of the megalith-tomb builders with other non-megalithic groups of our Neolithic settlers, and the use of the tomb builders' traditional skills in the development and construction of monuments that had previously been made of wood.

But these questions will take us too far away from the main theme of this short book. It is now time to review our main conclusions.

7

CONCLUSION

ALL that has been attempted in this small book is to try to define what we mean by a megalith and by megalithic architecture with special reference to western Europe, where this book will mainly be read, and which is an area so rich in megalithic monuments dating from prehistoric times. We have seen that numerically by far the most important type of megalithic monument is the chamber tomb and for most of this book we have been dealing with the chamber tombs of the Mediterranean, the western seaways of Atlantic Europe, and the north German–Scandinavian region. We have seen that archaeologists have held very widely differing views about the interrelations of the European chamber tombs. But it seems to me that in the present state of our knowledge the most likely and the most workable hypothesis about the European collective tombs involves the following three notions.

First that the custom of burying the dead by inhumation collectively in chamber tombs was in existence in the third millennium B.C. in the east Mediterranean. These early east Mediterranean chamber tombs were sometimes cut in the ground, but were elsewhere constructed above ground with dry-walled masonry and roofs of stone corbelling or of wood. The standard Minoan burial practice at all periods was collective interment in a family or communal ossuary used for many generations. There is no doubt that this practice, quite alien to the customs of the historic civilizations of Egypt, Mesopotamia, and the Anatolian plateau, was current and widespread in the east Mediterranean. It may, as Gordon Childe once suggested, even go farther back to Mesolithic times and to the cave-dwelling Natufians

128

Conclusion

of Palestine. But the ultimate origin of the collective tomb need not detain us much here, except that the east Mediterranean collective tomb could be an artificial version of the earlier collective burial tradition in a natural cave.

The Minoan collective tombs include natural caves, as well as rectangular stone chambers imitating two-roomed houses, and circular dry-walled enclosures usually called *tholoi*. There has been much dispute as to whether the Minoan *tholoi* were originally roofed by corbelling; some are as much as 30 to 40 feet across. None is corbel roofed at the present day; they might originally have been roofed by wood and thatch. The use collectively of natural caves in Crete dates from Early Minoan I through to Middle Minoan I (i.e. to the early second millennium); the best-known *tholoi* are those described by Xanthoudides and Droop and date from Early Minoan II through to Middle Minoan I; by Middle Minoan II, although collective burial in *tholoi* was still practised and additions were being made to existing tombs, there developed the custom of excavating small family tombs in the soft rock. It is not really our concern here to trace the origin of the Minoan dry-walled collective tombs; Sir Arthur Evans compared them with tombs in North Africa, but these Nubian and Libyan closed tombs are certainly later in date than the earliest Cretan *tholoi*. Other archaeologists have compared the *tholoi* with the circular brick-built structures discovered by Professor Mallowan at Arpachiyah; these certainly date from the fourth millennium B.C. – their purpose is still unknown, but they do not seem to have been tombs.

Suffice it here to insist that dry-walled and rock-cut collective tombs were being used in Minoan Crete in the second half of the third millennium B.C. Similar burial customs, as well as different ones, and similar constructional manifestations of these burial customs existed at the same time in the Cyclades. In these islands rough cupola tombs are found developing among slab-roofed cist-graves on sloping sites. In the southern islands of the Cyclades, like Melos, Amorgos, and Antiparos, there are shaft graves and built chamber tombs, but the earliest tombs appear to be trapezoid cists – yet even these were communal ossuaries and contained many skeletons. The northern group of islands, Syros and Andros, have interesting tombs, some being rectangular or oval and built by excavating in the hillside and roofing by corbelling. In neighbouring Euboea the tomb was sometimes a pit-cave, excavated in the ground, and the curious thing about these tombs and other morphological analogues is that they were used for single burials only. In Crete and perhaps in some other islands continuity in the use of rock-cut tombs for collective sepulchres can be observed between 1800 and 1500 B.C. and the great *tholoi* of the mainland of Greece are now dated between 1500 and 1350 B.C. They occur in the neighbourhood of Mycenae, such as the Treasury of Atreus itself; there are actually nine at Mycenae all plundered in antiquity. These Mycenaean *tholoi* are found mainly near the head of southward-facing gulfs and along natural trade routes by sea and land. There has been, as we have mentioned, great dispute about their origin and their relationships with many of the western European tombs we have been studying. Déchelette and others have seen Los Millares, Alcalá, New Grange, and Maes Howe as direct copies of the Mycenaean *tholoi*; recently Wolfel and Piggott have suggested that the whole process might be reversed and the Mycenaean *tholoi* be derived from the west. It seems to me, with many other archaeologists, that the mainland *tholoi* are an Aegean development of the Creto–Cycladic collective tombs, that is to say of the pre-Mycenaean Aegean collective tombs. The relationship of the developed passage graves and gallery graves of the West to the Mycenaean *tholoi* is thus a cousinly one; both represent parallel developments from the original Aegean collective tomb tradition of the end of the third millennium B.C. and the beginning of the second millennium. This does not mean that there were not cousinly relationships between the builders of these different tombs; we do now have good archaeological evidence of contacts between the

Conclusion

Mycenaean world and the Early Bronze Age people of southern Britain who developed the trade in British bronzes and Irish gold; and, as we have argued, the New Grange spirals surely take us straight back to Castelluccio, Hal Tarxien, and Mycenae.

This is then the first element in the threefold hypothesis we are setting out : the existence of collective-tomb burial in the Aegean in the third millennium, in contexts earlier than can be proved for collective burial in artificial tombs elsewhere in the Mediterranean and European world. The second element is the diffusion of the custom of collective burial, and its architectural expression in rock-cut and dry-walled tombs to the middle Mediterranean, to Iberia, and to southern France, and the development in these regions of a new architectural technique, of using megaliths for orthostatic walls and trabeate roofs. Megalithic chamber tombs then, as we understand them in western Europe, are translations into megalithic architecture of the east Mediterranean non-megalithic chamber tombs. It is also an inevitable concomitant of this hypothesis, or so it now seems to me, that this translation took place in at least three places, i.e. in Malta, in Iberia, and in southern France. In Sardinia and the Balearics the translation took place into cyclopean architecture, so that perhaps we should list five centres in the west Mediterranean in which early settlers from the east Mediterranean or their descendants began to evolve the traditions of megalithic and cyclopean architecture. The spread of the custom and practice of chamber tomb architecture from the west Mediterranean, Iberia, and southern France to the rest of France, the British Isles, and Scandinavia could then have manifested itself in many forms – the rock-cut tomb, the corbelled dry-walled vault, the megalithic chamber, the cyclopean tomb of *naveta*–giants' graves type, or any intermediate form between these. Actually the number of prehistoric rock-cut tombs in north-western Europe is negligible, and there are no cyclopean tombs known to me. The corbelled vaults like New Grange, Île Longue, Lochcrew, the Clava tombs, and

Maes Howe are most conspicuous by their rare occurrence. The great majority of European prehistoric collective tombs north of a line from Lisbon to Lyon are strictly megalithic; and only the megalithic form of construction gets to Denmark, Sweden, north Germany, and Holland; here there are no rock-cut or corbelled tombs.

The third element in the present hypothesis concerns the north European area. It does seem at the moment that when the builders of megalithic passage graves from western Europe arrived in Denmark they found, at least in south Jutland, people who were already practising a form of megalithic architecture; we do not need to recapitulate here the arguments in Chapter 3 about the origin of the *dös/dysse* type of monument. They were not collective tombs, but they were megalithic monuments.

If we accept this general hypothesis with its three basic premises, we accept the view that megalithic tomb architecture came into existence independently in several places in prehistoric Europe – at least in south Jutland, Malta, southern France, and southern Iberia. Many scholars, while accepting the independent origin of the *dös/dysse* type of monument in Denmark, still perhaps think in terms of one origin for megalithic architecture in the west Mediterranean, but it seems to me that in Iberia, in Malta, and in southern France the sequence from rock-cut (or dry-walled) tombs through elaborate megalithic tombs into smaller megalithic tombs is very difficult to disprove. Some would still like to see a native tradition of megalithic tomb building in existence in Iberia before the arrival of the east Mediterranean collective tomb builders; we have discussed this in Chapter 3, and it just may be so, but the fair assessment of the present state of our knowledge must be that no one has yet proved the chronological priority of these hypothetical 'dolmen-building' autochthones, and most of the available chronological evidence goes the other way. At the present, then, the 'dolmens' of Iberia and France cannot be given a role like the *dös/dysse* tombs in Denmark.

Conclusion

And, of course, if we accept the view that in Europe itself megalithic architecture could originate in four separate places, there is really no need to worry our heads unduly about the presence of megalithic structures in Algeria, Palestine, India, or Japan. The use of megaliths for constructional purposes was obviously developed in the world at different times by different people for different purposes. When we forget this common fact of the use of large stones and concentrate on the details of use, date, and form, the resemblances between megalithic monuments in different parts of the world disappear. Maps which purport to show the world-wide distribution of megalithic monuments are in fact doing no more than that, and show no cultural or chronological unity; they are as valuable and as misleading as a world-wide distribution map of rock-cut tombs or corbelled vaults. Once we appreciate this point we cease, of course, to talk about a megalithic people or a megalithic race. If there is no necessary cultural or chronological or functional link between all megalithic monuments, how much less should we expect the builders of these diverse monuments, divorced from each other in time and place, to be of one physical type. The 'megalithic race' like the Ancient Egyptians or the Phoenicians or any other of the Master Races who were supposed to have girdled the earth with civilization are gone; and a very good thing too. For too long they bedevilled our understanding of the megalithic problem, because in the end there is no megalithic 'problem', only many problems – the problems of megalithic architecture in many different areas and periods.

Here we have been concerned with one area and one time – western Europe between 2500 and 1000 B.C. The main answer to this problem is the spread of chamber tombs and collective burial from the east Mediterranean to the west, and the diffusion of the megalithic version of these tombs through western Europe. It is easy to talk of this spread and diffusion; these are archaeological forms of speech. It is less easy to try and speak historically about what we think is implied by this 'spread'. Many different interpretations of the historical fact behind the spread of megalithic tombs in Europe have been put forward. Perry and Elliot Smith saw the builders of the megalith tombs as prospectors looking for metal and indeed for any other sources that might be called 'Givers of Life'; others have seen them as some sort of travelling undertakers persuading the natives to adopt a new style of tomb; other archaeologists have likened the spread of tombs to the spread of a religion and compared the differences in tomb types to the differences in Christian religious architecture between, say, Amiens Cathedral and a Wesleyan Methodist Chapel in Carmarthenshire. Other archaeologists regarded the spread of megalithic tombs as the result of an ordinary colonial movement.

I do not think that the answer is a clear-cut one in the terms of any particular theory; in the absence of written evidence we may go on arguing for ever about the historical role of the megalith builders, and there may indeed be an element of truth in all the theories. Each writer must try to convey his own mixture of prospectors, undertakers, missionaries, colonists. It seems to me useful to think of the migrations of a group of people who did the movement of the megalith builders in reverse and in historical times; and I refer to the Vikings. We know of their movements from literary sources and we know the reasons that lay behind their movements – shortage of food, overpopulation, a search for wealth. We know, too, fairly precise details of how they set out – their boats, who were in them, what equipment they took. I do not suggest for one moment that this parallel of the Vikings should be pushed very far, but our knowledge of the Viking movements can be usefully at the back of our mind as we try to visualize the megalith builders.

The first great sea-rovers in ancient history that we know about were the Minoans, who preceded the Greeks and the Phoenicians in their domination of the Mediterranean. The spark that set off the development of collective-tomb architecture in western Europe, in all its variety and complication, was most probably the arrival of Minoans or Aegeans in the middle and west Mediterranean from the east. Maybe they arrived as little more than traders, with perhaps no women and therefore no potters, just boat-loads of men looking for a place to live and to exploit, metals to mine – precursors of those voyages which we know took place five hundred years later (or less) when Mycenaean colonists and traders left pottery in Malta, Sicily, southern Italy, the Lipari Islands, and in the bay of Ischia, and, both of them, Minoan and Mycenaean precursors of the later Phoenicians and Greeks. It has been argued[1] that there was no movement westwards from the east Mediterranean until Middle Minoan II times and it may therefore be 2000 to 1900 B.C. when we should date our earliest rock-cut tombs in Sicily, Malta, Portugal, and Sardinia, our earliest dry-walled collective tombs in southern Spain.

We should not suppose that these early voyagers took much, if any, longer to cross the Mediterranean than did their Phoenician and Greek successors; the settlement at Los Millares may have been being laid out six weeks after an adventurous boat-load of men set out from the Aegean. The old phrase, 'Allow a hundred years for this culture to spread across the Mediterranean and another hundred for it to spread across France' are now old-fashioned parodies of archaeological interpretation, which forgot that the spread of tombs is the movement of men who built them, and that there is no reason to insist that the man who traded a faience bead to Brittany took longer to cross France from Narbonne than did the men who in Greek times brought tin from Corbilo, that is to say, four weeks. Nor should we suppose that these trading and colonial movements were unitary, were all associated with collective tombs, or took place at one moment. They were probably spread over a long time, with renewed contacts, and

1. H. J. Kantor, 'The Aegean and the Orient in the Second Millennium B.C.' in *American Journal of Archaeology*, 1947. (*Special volume.*)

movements in reverse. Bernabò Brea's analysis of the Siculan I period showed the interaction of collective tomb building and non-collective tomb building cultures all deriving from the Aegean; and in the Chalcolithic of France we have seen the same thing – the statue-menhirs of southeastern France and the *symbolkeramik* of western France.

The Middle Minoan II westward movement of Miss Kantor may not be the beginning of the Aegean contacts with the west Mediterranean; the beginnings may well go back before 2000 and 1900 B.C., were reinforced in Middle Minoan II, and continued, perhaps sporadically, perhaps uninterrupted, until the undisputed contacts of Mycenaean times and the trade in faience beads. There has too often been a tendency to date 'the spread' of collective tombs, when it may well be series of events over a long period of time. The Vikings are one good historical parallel; the Mediterranean colonization of the Greeks and Phoenicians is another good one; and how close in southern Iberia are the collective-tomb centres to those the later historical people developed! The spread of Mohammedanism into Iberia might be another good historical parallel; and how close are the great Iberian megaliths in the south to the great Mohammedan centres! Certainly religion played an important part in the life of the original megalith builders, even if I cannot see them myself as primarily missionaries. It was a powerful, compelling, Aegean-inspired religion that made them build their tombs (or their tomb temples?) with such labour, and preserve in various ways the image of their tutelary and funerary goddess. The goddess figure, the axe, the horns, and other symbols take us back again from the Paris Basin, from Gavrinnis, from Anghelu Ruju to Crete, the Aegean, even Troy. It cannot be disputed that a powerful religion of east Mediterranean origin informed and inspired the builders of the megalithic tombs as they spread through western Europe. Yet it seems to me unlikely that religion was the driving force of their migrations; rather it was the solace of their exile in the far west and north of Europe. They were surely first looking for

Conclusion

new places to live, new materials for life, and perhaps also trade. I think that among the materials for which they were looking metals were one, and to this extent Perry and Elliot Smith were right with their prospectors. Surely this is why their settlements were in Almeria, in Ireland, in Anglesey, and in southern Brittany. We can summarize this discussion, then, by saying it is reasonable to suppose the primary driving force of the megalith builders was a colonial and trading one and a prospecting one, and that this colonization or prospection (and in a certain way the megalith builders discovered western Europe) was carried out by people with a strong religious faith and a complicated funerary practice.[1]

Are the megalith builders, then, the people who introduced metallurgy to western Europe? and even if not so, why, when many of the tombs overlap with metal-using economies in parts of Europe, are there so few metal objects in the thousands of megalithic tombs? We know that the arts of metallurgy were flourishing in the Aegean world that we suggest gave birth to these voyages to the west, and the people who buried their dead at Alcalá and Los Millares were metal-using. Equally certain is the fact that the Maltese megaliths have no metal in them, and that metal is extremely rare in the two thousand British megaliths. We are faced with a dilemma – the contemporaneity of metal-using societies and the megalith builders and the derivation of the megalith builders of France and

1. In his last book, *The Prehistory of European Society* (Penguin Books, 1958), the late Professor Gordon Childe has thought again about the interpretation of megalithic tombs, and decided to compare the spread of these tombs with the spread of Christian religion by the Celtic 'saints' in the post-Roman period. This is an intriguing and surprising idea, and it will come as a shock to some to read in Childe's book of 'the megalithic saints'. The present writer prefers a more prosaic (and perhaps more profane) interpretation of the role of the megalith builders in terms of prospectors, traders, colonists, and metal-workers, without underestimating the prestige and power they must have had as bearers of a new religion, practisers of a new burial custom, and no mean funerary architects.

the British Isles and Scandinavia from Iberian societies which were metal-using. And there is more to it than this; some of the megalithic tombs are definitely in metalliferous regions. The passage graves of the Hérault in southern France are in a copper-bearing area; they contain no metal objects, but fine flint copies of western European copper daggers. Then surely the magnificent polished stone axes in many Breton tombs are ritual copies of metal axes and made by a people who knew the use of metal. Some years ago Mr T. G. E. Powell and I suggested that the absence of metal from British and Breton megaliths was 'for some sociological reason'. I still believe this, and suggest that some of these settlers were metal prospectors who traded metal back to the Mediterranean, and who did not bury finished metal tools in their tombs but stone copies of them.

I have said 'some of these settlers' most deliberately. In a paper written twenty years ago and of which this book is a reconsideration, I used the phrase the 'Dual Nature of the Megalithic Colonization of Europe', and by that I meant mainly the formalization of the idea so clearly set out by Gordon Childe years before, namely that as far as north-western Europe was concerned there were two main patterns in the spread of megalithic tombs, the passage graves and the gallery graves. We have seen in this book that that idea, while still very useful, was an oversimplification, and that all the main varieties of megalithic tomb go back to the same basic form of rock-cut and dry-walled Mediterranean tomb. But there is another sense in which we can still speak of the dual nature of the megalithic colonization of western Europe. It is in the sense of distinguishing the primary east Mediterranean inspired colonists who were, we believe, *inter alia* metal prospectors, and the non-primary tomb builders of western and northern Europe who might well be autochtones who adopted the impressive form of tomb and the custom of burial and a religion at first, second, or third hand from the primary colonists. We are becoming used to speaking of secondary Neolithic culture; I think we can talk of the secondary aspect of the megalithic colonization of western Europe and that many of our megalithic tomb cultures could most properly be described as secondary Chalcolithic.

The tombs of the Paris Basin or of the Severn–Cotswold and Clyde–Carlingford groups must surely owe their explanation in historical terms to small groups of settlers coming to live in a countryside already occupied by Neolithic societies (or even societies that were the results of acculturation between Mesolithic and Neolithic groups); the fundamental economy of these groups, as of so many of the megalith builders of southern France, has nothing to do with the primary prospection and discovery of the Mediterranean tomb builders, but is an agricultural or pastoral economy whose main roots are non-megalithic.

If we cannot say that the megalith builders, or at least some of them – the primary passage-grave builders – did not introduce metallurgy into north-western Europe in the sense that they set going a continuous tradition of metalworking, surely it is in the wake of their pioneer colonization that the metal industries of Ireland and Britain came into existence. To a certain extent, then, we could say that the development of metal-working in the British Isles was in part a secondary aspect of the megalithic colonization of these areas. This is perhaps tantamount to saying that the passage-grave builders may have been in part responsible for the beginning of metal-working in western Europe.

To solve this complicated problem we need to know more of the settlement sites of the megalith builders. We do have some of them – Los Millares, Vila Nova de San Pedro, Fontbouïsse, Le Lizo, and they all have metal in them. Our English and Irish contemporary settlements – Clegyr Boia, Lough Gur, for example – do not have metal. It is perhaps in Scandinavia that we may solve the problem of the nature of the passage-grave settlers. Here, if we agree that the passage graves represent a settlement from the west, we ought to be able to isolate the material culture, if any, of the first settlers. There are many Danish settlements of the early passage-grave period, but they reveal a native culture; were the people who arrived in Jutland and the islands and produced a historical situation that resulted in the construction of large stone tombs no more than boat-loads of men from Brittany or Spain?

In our brief discussion of what is meant by the spread of tombs it is possible to forget that behind these movements there are not only people, but human beings who were intrepid navigators, who survived the first navigational shocks of leaving the tideless Mediterranean and cabotage, for the rigours of the four hundred miles of storm and sea between Finisterre in north-west Spain and Finistère in western Brittany; these people must indeed have thought at times that they were journeying to the ends of the earth. In what ships did they battle with the Atlantic breakers and the tides of the Bay of Biscay? Certainly not in dug-out canoes; even with outriggers they would be no craft for the Atlantic. As Shetelig and Brøgger have so cogently argued in their book *The Viking Ships*, there were two early traditions of boat-building in Scandinavia, namely the skin-boat which was seaworthy and the dug-out which was not. We can perhaps see the megalithic navigators in skin-boats, or in wooden examplars of these skin-boats, and it is this type of boat, as Lethbridge has argued, which may survive in forms of modern boats on the west Atlantic seaboard like the Portuguese *saveiros*.

One last question: How many people were involved in the primary megalithic colonization, and what effect, if any, did they have on the ethnic population of their day and afterwards? The numbers of the tombs are no real guide, because we do not know if they represented the tombs of all the population concerned or only chiefs and religious leaders, and, if we accept the secondary aspect of the megalithic colonization, many of the people buried in the 'dolmens' on the *causses* country of the south of France, for example, were a continuing native pastoral population which adopted megalithic architecture and collective burial. There is no megalithic race, as we have said, but it does appear likely that the physical type which spread with the primary colonization was mainly a Mediterranean long-headed type, with, as well, some round-headed 'Prospectors'. Linguistic and archaeological correlations are notoriously dangerous and attractive, but in a welter of theory and confusion about the linguistic labelling of prehistoric and protohistoric people it seems certain that the megalith builders did not speak an Indo-European language. We should expect them to speak a Mediterranean language, some pre-Indo-European language which may have survived to the present day as Berber or as Basque. But whatever they spoke, and whatever they looked like – and my guess is that a group of men round a café table in Brest or a fishing-boat in St Jean de Luz harbour or a pelota court at San Sebastian might quite well represent those intrepid navigators who with relief anchored in Quiberon or Dublin Bay four thousand years ago after their rough crossing from Iberia – the megalith builders surely formed a most important, as well as a most exciting, element in the early history of western Europe. It is at once the fascination and the frustration of prehistoric archaeology that what we can say about them is so full of doubts and disputes. This book has not sought to resolve those doubts or add to those disputes, but to set out what various views exist and what seems a possible point of view to adopt until fresh researches force its modification or abandonment.

ADDENDUM: CARBON 14 DATING

SINCE this book was first written, Carbon 14 dates have been published from many Neolithic contexts and a few megalithic contexts in Europe. These alter the chronology suggested in this book from archaeological methods practised before the advent of Carbon 14 dating. It is still too early to produce a completely revised megalithic chronology from Carbon 14 dates but the following observations should and must be made now.

In the first place it is now clear that the chronology current for the beginning of the Neolithic in north-western Europe, as set out for example in Professor Piggott's *Neolithic Cultures of the British Isles* (1954), is too short. The beginnings of the Neolithic in northern France, Ireland, and Britain would now seem to be between 3500 and 3000 B.C. It would also seem that some at least of the earliest megalithic monuments may go back to this period. Many of these new Carbon 14 dates for megaliths and associated cultures have been published in *Antiquity* in the last two years (*Antiquity*, 1959, p. 289; 1960, pp. 100, 147, 212; 1961, pp. 143, 147). These and other dates not yet published suggest now the following reflections on the chronology set out in this book when first written in 1958.

1. The *floruit* of passage graves in Northern Europe (p. 60) referred to as the first half of the second millennium should now be extended backwards to include the second half of the third millennium. It is possible that passage graves in northern Europe were in existence as early as 2700 B.C. and it seems certain that

the *floruit* of megalithic tombs in Holland may be dated between 2800 and 2200 B.C.

2. We have quoted the Leisners as saying that the first phase of Los Millares I was before 1800 B.C. It is now clear from Carbon 14 dating that the international bell beakers are to be dated at 2200 B.C. or thereabouts. Los Millares I was well before this. A Carbon 14 dated of 2345 B.C. from Los Millares dates the end of Phase I. The beginning of Los Millares may be five hundred or more years before, as is suggested on archaeological grounds by Dr Blance (*Antiquity*, 1961, p. 192).

3. Professor J. D. Evans had suggested on archaeological correlation grounds the date of 2100 B.C. for his I B Phase in Malta. The first Carbon 14 date for a prehistoric phase in Malta, from the floor of the smaller of the two megalithic temples at Ta Hagrat, Mgarr, gave a date of 2700 B.C. (For this see Evans, *Antiquity*, 1960, to be read in conjunction with Brea, *Antiquity*, 1960, p. 132, Evans, *Antiquity*, 1960, p. 218, and Trump, *Antiquity*, 1960, p. 300.)

4. In Brittany the two passage graves of the Île Carn and Les Sept Îles have given Carbon 14 dates that suggest they were built between 3500 and 3000 B.C. and contemporary material from a near-by settlement at Curnic, also in Finistère, was dated to the same period (see Giot in *Antiquity*, 1960, p. 147, and 1961, p. 147).

5. In Ireland three Carbon 14 dates suggest that the passage grave in the Mound of the Hostages at Tara was built probably about 2100 B.C. (For a discussion of these dates and other Carbon 14 dates from Ireland see Watts, *Antiquity*, 1950, p. 111.) In Britain, while we have as yet no Carbon 14 dates from megalithic tombs we have dates from unchambered long barrows like Nutbane and from Windmill Hill itself; from this it seems now likely that a monument like West Kennet was built between 3000 and 2500 B.C. The

Addendum : Carbon 14 Dating

date quoted above (p. 119) for the *floruit* of the Severn–Cotswold tombs and of Irish passage graves as between 2000 and 1700 B.C. is clearly too late. (On the problem of the dating of the British Neolithic from Carbon 14 dates see Clark and Godwin, *Antiquity*, 1962, p. 10.)

It is still too early to be dogmatic about the details of a new megalithic chronology; we do need many more dates from many more sites in the next five years. But it is not too early to say that our earlier chronology was too short and that we must now think of megalithic tombs as in existence in Iberia and part of north-western Europe as early as 3000 B.C. and probably three or four hundred years earlier. This does not mean that all megalithic tombs were built then; we know Tara was built in 2100 B.C. and other tombs a thousand years later. But it does mean that megalithic tombs were being built and used in western Europe from perhaps 3500 B.C. to 1000 B.C. This should not surprise us; our own Christian burial custom of inhumation in a flat grave has lasted for two thousand years. It does suggest however that the role of the megalith builders in areas like western France, Ireland, and northern Scotland, for example, may be more important than we had hitherto thought.

These Carbon 14 dates are not yet enough for us to resolve with certainty the problem of the origins of passage graves in Iberia and France, and the relations of these early monuments to the strictly megalithic monuments of north Portugal and the collective tombs of the east Mediterranean. The resolution of these problems will be one of the excitements of prehistoric archaeology in the next five to ten years, and will be perhaps even more exciting than our realization in the last four years that our absolute dating of the earliest west- and north-European megaliths had been wrong. We live at the moment, as regards the absolute chronology of prehistoric Europe, in a remarkable period of change because of the arrival of the technique of Carbon 14 dating. Even now it is being proposed that a new half-life formula for Carbon 14 should be adopted which means that the dates for the third millennium B.C. quoted here will have to be made earlier by between 150 and 200 years.

G. E. D.

March 1962

BOOKS FOR FURTHER READING

WE have already said that there are, surprisingly, only two books in the English language dealing in a general way with the subject of the present book; both were published a long time ago and are out of print. James Fergusson's *Rude Stone Monuments in all Countries: their Age and Uses* was published in 1872, and T. Eric Peet's *Rough Stone Monuments and their Builders* in 1912. Among classic nineteenth-century statements of megalithic theory and controversy we should mention Baron Bonstetten's *Essai sur les dolmens* (Geneva, 1865) and Oscar Montelius's *Orient und Europa,* first published as '*Orienten och Europa*' in *Antiqvarisk Tidskrift for Sverige,* 1905. There are, however, several articles in learned journals dealing in a general way with the problems concerned, and the following five should be read :

1. Peake and Fleure, 'Megaliths and Beakers', in the *Journal of the Royal Anthropological Institute,* vol. IX, 1930.
2. C. Daryll Forde, 'The Early Cultures of Atlantic Europe', in the *American Anthropologist,* vol. 32, 1930.
3. C. A. Nordman, 'The Megalithic Culture of Northern Europe', in *Finska Fornminnesforeningens Tidskrift,* vol. 39, 1935. (This is really a book, and is in English.)
4. V. G. Childe, 'Scottish Megalithic Tombs and their Affinities', in *Transactions of the Glasgow Archaeological Society,* vol. III, 1932.
5. G. E. Daniel, 'The Dual Nature of the Megalithic Colonization of Prehistoric Europe', in *Proceedings of the Prehistoric Society,* vol. VII, 1941.

The Megalith Builders of Western Europe

The story of the megalith builders of western Europe is part of the general story of prehistoric culture in Europe between 2500 and 1000 B.C., and for this period we have two excellent guides for the general reader: V. Gordon Childe's *The Dawn of European Civilization*, first published in 1925, and of which the current (sixth) edition is 1957, and C. F. C. Hawkes's *The Prehistoric Foundations of Europe* (1940). A good picture is also provided in Peake and Fleure, *The Way of the Sea* (1929) and in (Sir) Mortimer Wheeler, *The Prehistoric Era in the West*, in Eyre, *European Civilization, its Origin and Development* (1942). Gordon Childe's *Prehistoric Migrations in Europe* (Oslo, 1950) has much to say about megaliths, and so has Dorothy Davison's *The Story of Prehistoric Civilizations* (1951). (Sir) Thomas Kendrick's *The Axe Age* (1925) was a pioneer study of modern megalithic problems.

*

Chapters 1 and 2. On Japanese megaliths see Gowland, 'Dolmens and Burial Mounds of Japan', *Archaeologia*, vol. 55. The views of Wheeler and Childe on Indian megaliths will be found in two articles in *Ancient India*, No. 4 (1947–8); Wheeler's 'Brahmagiri and Chandravalli, 1947: Megalithic and Other Cultures in Mysore State', and Childe's 'Megaliths'. On Stonehenge and stone circles in general see R. J. C. Atkinson, *Stonehenge* (1956), and Atkinson, Piggott, and Sandars, *Excavations at Dorchester, Oxon* (1951).

Chapter 3. The best account of the Scandinavian sequence to set the problem in its European setting is still Nordman's 1935 article already cited. Becker's views were first set out in his *Mosefundne Lerkar fra Yngre Stenalder: Studier Over Tragbaegerkulturen i Denmark* (Copenhagen, 1948) which has an English summary. See also O. Klindt-Jensen's *Denmark* (1958). On the Iberian megaliths see E. T. Leeds, 'The Dolmens and Megalithic Tombs of Spain and Portugal', in *Archaeologia*, vol. 70, 1918–20; C. Daryll

Books for Further Reading

Forde, 'The Megalithic Culture Sequence in Iberia', Liverpool *Annals of Archaeology and Anthropology*, vol. XVI, 1929. On beakers see M. A. Smith 'Iberian Beakers', *Proceedings of the Prehistoric Society*, vol. XIX, 1953. The views of the Leisners are set out in Georg and Vera Leisner, *Die Megalithgraber der Iberischen Halbinsel* (Berlin, 1943 and 1956) and in their *Anta do Concelho de Reguengos de Monsaraz* (Lisbon, 1951); see also Marquez and G. and V. Leisner *Las Sepulcros Megaliticos de Huelva* (Madrid, 1952). The last two books are studied critically by S. Piggott in his 'The Tholos Tomb in Iberia', *Antiquity*, vol. XXVII, 1953. Wolfel's views are discussed by Sir John Myres in his 'Cupola Tombs in the Aegean and in Iberia', in *Antiquity*, vol. XXVII, 1953. The north-eastern Spanish province is dealt with admirably in Pericot y García's *Los Sepulcros Megaliticos Catalanes y la Cultura Pirenaica* (Barcelona, 1950).

Chapter 4. Still the best account of Italian prehistory is T. E. Peet, *The Stone and Bronze Ages in Italy*, published in 1909, to be supplemented by Gervasio *I Dolmen e la Civilta del Bronzo nelle Puglie* (1913). On the western Mediterranean as a whole see E. T. Leeds 'Problems of Megalithic Architecture in the western Mediterranean' in Liverpool *Annals of Archaeology and Anthropology*, vol. IX, 1922. On Sicily and the Liparis see Bernabò Brea, 'The Prehistoric Culture Sequence in Sicily' in *Annual Reports*, University of London Institute of Archaeology, 1950, and his *Sicily before the Greeks*, 1957. On Malta, T. Zammit, 'The Prehistoric Remains of the Maltese Islands', *Antiquity*, vol. IV, 1930; J. B. Ward-Perkins, 'Problems of Maltese Prehistory', *Antiquity*, vol. XVI, 1942; J. D. Evans, 'The Prehistoric Culture Sequence in the Maltese Archipelago', *Proceedings of the Prehistoric Society*, vol. XIX, 1953, and his *Malta* (1959). The current views on the Sardinian material may be read in M. Pallottino, *La Sardegna Nuragica* (Rome, 1950) and C. Zervos, *La Civilisation de la Sardaigne du début de l'eneolithique à la fin de la période nouragique* (Paris, 1954). For the Balearics see W. J. Hemp's articles in *Archaeologia*, vol. 76, 1927, and the *Antiquaries Journal*, vols. 12 (1927) and 13 (1928).

Chapter 5. Most of the material on the megaliths of France is in periodicals; see particularly Le Rouzic's articles on the Breton megaliths in *L'Anthropologie* for 1933 and 1934, and J. Arnal's 'Presentacion de dolmenes y estaciones del departamento del Hérault' in *Ampurias*, vols. XVI–XVII, 1953–4, and G. E. Daniel, 'The Allée Couvertes of France' in the *Archaeological Journal*, vol. CXII, 1956. For more full general treatment see G. Bailloud and P. Mieg de Boofzheim, *Les Civilisations néolithiques de la France dans leur contexte européen*, 1955, and G. E. Daniel, *The Prehistoric Chamber Tombs of France*, 1960.

Chapter 6. For the general background of British prehistory see Grahame Clark, *Prehistoric England* (first published, 1940), Jacquetta and Christopher Hawkes, *Prehistoric Britain* (1958), V. Gordon Childe, *Prehistoric Communities of the British Isles* (1940), S. Piggott, *British Prehistory* (1949), Joseph Raftery, *Prehistoric Ireland* (1951), and S. P. ÓRíordáin, *Antiquities of the Irish Countryside* (1953). For more detailed treatment of megalithic problems see G. E. Daniel, *The Prehistoric Chamber Tombs of England and Wales* (1950) and S. Piggott, *The Neolithic Cultures of the British Isles* (1954); W. F. Grimes, 'The Megalithic Monuments of Wales', in *Proceedings of the Preshistoric Society*, 1936; O. G. S. Crawford, *The Long Barrows of the Cotswolds*, 1925; T. G. E. Powell, 'The Passage Graves of Ireland' in *Proceedings of the Prehistoric Society*, 1938; Powell and Daniel, *Barclodiad y Gawres*, 1956; and S. Piggott, *The West Kennet Long Barrow Excavation 1955–6*, 1961.

INDEX

Index

152

Index

Index

Thomas, H. H., 18
Tibradden, 114
Tinkinswood, 17, 118, 120
Transepted gallery graves, 105, 120, 121
Tressé, 43
Troels-Smith, J., 57
Troy, 81, 83
Typology, 65

Ur, Royal Tombs at, 31

V-shaped passage graves, 42, 44, 64, 65, 80

Valera, R. de, 123–4
Vikings, 32, 59, 134–6, 140

Wedge-shaped galleries, 43, 44, 124
Wessex Bronze Age, 115
Wheeler, Sir Mortimer, 23, 25, 148
Windmill Hill Culture, 119
Wölfel, D. J., 78, 130
Wood, 11, 27, 36
Worsaae, J. J. A., 54–5

Zammit, Sir Themistocles, 85